soups

soups

MURDOCH BOOKS

contents

soup kitchen

Someone once said 'Soup is cuisine's kindest course'. Soup soothes us when we're ill, feeds us when we're short on time (or money!), curtain-raises at our dinner parties and provides the best use possible for almost any seasonal produce.

Soup spans seasons, continents and the whole gamut of ingredients and cooking skills. Soups can be hot or chilled and can even take us travelling to exotic places; to Vietnam, Tunisia, Thailand or Spain. It is suited to any occasion and comes in a mind-boggling number of colours, consistencies and textures. It can be as familiar a friend as a creamy pumpkin purée, a thick clam chowder or cheesy French onion soup — menu stalwarts that are never out of vogue.

A soup can have the suave sophistication of classic crab bisque, or be as down-home rustic as pasta and bean or pea and ham. These may be fashioned from humble everyday staples but they're the soups we arguably most love to cook and eat.

Soup loves an accompaniment or two (rolls, dumplings, toast or croutons) but is equally happy served solo. In fact, the only thing that soup really isn't capable of doing is making itself. Lucky for you, the eager soup cooks of the world, here are all your favourite soup recipes in one indispensable volume.

classic

French onion soup

50 g (1¾ oz) butter
750 g (1 lb 10 oz) onions, finely sliced
2 garlic cloves, finely chopped
45 g (1½ oz/⅓ cup) plain (all-purpose) flour
2 litres (70 fl oz/8 cups) beef or chicken stock
250 ml (9 fl oz/1 cup) dry white wine
1 bay leaf
2 thyme sprigs
12 slices stale baguette
100 g (3½ oz) Gruyère cheese, finely grated

Melt the butter in a heavy-based saucepan and add the onion. Cook over low heat, stirring occasionally, for 25 minutes, or until the onion is deep golden brown and beginning to caramelise.

Add the garlic and flour and stir continuously for 2 minutes. Gradually blend in the stock and the wine, stirring continuously, and bring to the boil. Add the bay leaf and thyme and season. Cover the pan and simmer for 25 minutes. Remove the bay leaf and thyme. Preheat the grill (broiler).

Toast the baguette slices, then divide among six soup bowls. Ladle the soup over the top and sprinkle with the grated cheese. Grill (broil) until the cheese melts and turns light golden brown. Serve immediately.

SERVES 6

Lentil and silverbeet soup

Chicken stock

1 kg (2 lb 8 oz) chicken
    trimmings (neck, ribs, wings),
    fat removed
1 small onion, roughly chopped
1 bay leaf
3–4 flat-leaf (Italian) parsley
    sprigs
1–2 oregano or thyme sprigs

280 g (10 oz) brown lentils
850 g (1 lb 14 oz) silverbeet
    (Swiss chard)
3 tablespoons olive oil
1 large onion, finely chopped
4 garlic cloves, crushed
25g (1 oz) coriander (cilantro)
    leaves, finely chopped
4 tablespoons lemon juice
lemon wedges, to serve

To make the stock, put all the ingredients in a large saucepan. Add 3 litres
(102 fl oz/12 cups) of water and bring to the boil. Skim any scum from the
surface. Reduce the heat and simmer for 2 hours. Strain the stock, discarding
the trimmings, onion and herbs. Chill overnight. You will need about 1 litre
(35 fl oz/4 cups).

Skim any fat from the stock. Put the lentils in a large saucepan, add the stock and
1 litre (35 fl oz/4 cups) of water. Bring to the boil, then reduce the heat and simmer,
covered, for 1 hour.

Meanwhile, remove the stems from the silverbeet and shred the leaves. Heat the
oil in a saucepan over medium heat and cook the onion for 2–3 minutes, or until
transparent. Add the garlic and cook for 1 minute. Add the silverbeet and toss for
2–3 minutes, or until wilted. Stir the mixture into the lentils. Add the coriander
and lemon juice, season, and simmer, covered for 15–20 minutes. Serve with
lemon wedges.

SERVES 6

Pumpkin soup

500 ml (17 fl oz/2 cups) vegetable stock
750 g (1 lb 10 oz) butternut pumpkin (squash),
    cut into 1.5 cm ($5/8$ inch) cubes
2 onions, chopped
2 garlic cloves, halved
1/4 teaspoon ground nutmeg
3 tablespoons pouring (whipping) cream

Put the stock and 500 ml (17 fl oz/2 cups) of water in a large heavy-based saucepan and bring to the boil. Add the pumpkin, onion and garlic and return to the boil. Reduce the heat slightly and cook for 15 minutes, or until the pumpkin is soft.

Drain the vegetables in a colander, reserving the liquid. Purée the pumpkin mixture in a blender until smooth (you may need to add some of the reserved liquid). Return the pumpkin purée to the pan and stir in enough of the reserved liquid to reach the desired consistency.

Serve with cream swirled on top and season to taste with nutmeg, salt and pepper.

SERVES 4

Spring vegetable
soup with basil pesto

1.25 litres (44 fl oz/5 cups) vegetable or chicken stock
1 tablespoon extra virgin olive oil
8 spring onions (scallions), finely sliced
2 celery stalks, finely sliced
12 baby (dutch) carrots, sliced
310 g (11 oz) asparagus, woody ends removed,
    cut into 3 cm (1¼ inch) lengths
150 g (5½ oz) baby corn, cut into 3 cm (1¼ inch) lengths
60 g (2¼ oz/¼ cup) fresh or bottled pesto
extra virgin olive oil, to thin pesto (see Note)
shaved parmesan cheese, to garnish

Bring the stock to the boil in a large saucepan. Meanwhile, heat the olive oil in a large heavy-based saucepan and add the spring onion and celery. Cover and cook over medium heat for 5 minutes, or until softened.

Add the stock to the spring onion mixture and mix well. Add the carrot, asparagus and corn to the pan. Return the mixture to the boil, then reduce the heat and simmer for 10 minutes.

Top with a dollop of pesto, season to taste, and garnish with shaved parmesan.

SERVES 4

NOTE: Homemade pesto or fresh pesto from a deli will give a better flavour than bottled pesto. If you prefer a thinner pesto, mix it with a little olive oil to give it a runnier consistency.

Crab bisque

50 g (1¾ oz) butter
½ carrot, finely chopped
½ onion, finely chopped
1 celery stalk, finely chopped
1 bay leaf
2 thyme sprigs
1 kg (2 lb 4 oz) live crabs,
   cleaned and claws detached

2 tablespoons tomato paste
   (concentrated purée)
2 tablespoons brandy
150 ml (5 fl oz) dry white wine
1 litre (35 fl oz/4 cups) fish stock
60 g (2¼ oz) rice
3 tablespoons thick
   (double/heavy) cream
¼ teaspoon cayenne pepper

Heat the butter in a large saucepan. Add the vegetables, bay leaf and thyme and cook over medium heat for 3 minutes, without allowing the vegetables to colour. Add the crab claws, legs and bodies and cook for 5 minutes, or until the crab shells turn red. Add the tomato paste, brandy and white wine and simmer for 2 minutes, or until reduced by half.

Add the stock and 500 ml (17 fl oz/2 cups) of water and bring to the boil. Reduce the heat and simmer for 5 minutes. Remove the shells, leaving the crab meat in the stock, and reserve the claws to use as a garnish. Finely crush the shells in a mortar and pestle (or in a food processor with a little of the stock).

Return the crushed shells to the soup with the rice. Bring to the boil, reduce the heat, cover and simmer for about 20 minutes, or until the rice is soft.

Immediately strain the bisque into a clean saucepan through a fine sieve lined with damp muslin, pressing down firmly on the solids to extract all the liquid. Add the cream and season with salt and cayenne pepper, then gently reheat. Garnish with the crab claws.

SERVES 4

Spinach soup

30 g (1 oz) butter
1 onion, finely chopped
500 g (1 lb 2 oz) floury potatoes, grated
1 litre (35 fl oz/4 cups) vegetable or chicken stock
500 g (1 lb 2 oz) frozen chopped English spinach
¼ teaspoon ground nutmeg
sour cream, to serve

Melt the butter in a large saucepan over medium heat. Add the chopped onion and cook, stirring occasionally, until soft but not browned.

Add the potato and stock to the pan and mix well, scraping the onion from the bottom of the pan. Add the unthawed blocks of spinach and cook, covered, until the spinach has thawed and broken up, stirring occasionally. Uncover and simmer, stirring often, for 10–15 minutes, or until the potato is very soft. Transfer to a blender or food processor and blend in batches until smooth.

Return the soup to the pan and gently reheat. Add the nutmeg and season. Serve with sour cream swirled on top.

SERVES 4

Chicken and vegetable soup

1.5 kg (3 lb 5 oz) chicken
1 onion
2 large leeks, halved lengthwise
  and well washed
3 large celery stalks
5 black peppercorns
1 bay leaf
2 large carrots, peeled and
  diced

1 large swede (rutabaga),
  peeled and diced
2 large tomatoes, peeled,
  seeded and finely chopped
165 g (5¾ oz/¾ cup) barley
1 tablespoon tomato paste
  (concentrated purée)
2 tablespoons finely chopped
  flat-leaf (Italian) parsley

Put the chicken, onion, 1 leek, 1 celery stalk, halved, the peppercorns and bay leaf in a large saucepan and add enough water to cover. Bring to the boil, then reduce the heat and simmer for 1½ hours, skimming any impurities that rise to the surface.

Strain the stock through a fine sieve and return to the cleaned saucepan. Discard the onion, leek, celery, peppercorns and bay leaf, and set the chicken aside to cool slightly. Discard the fat and bones, then shred the flesh. Cover with plastic wrap and refrigerate.

Allow the stock to cool, then refrigerate overnight. Skim the fat from the surface. Put the stock in a large saucepan and bring to the boil. Dice the remaining leek and celery and add to the soup with the carrot, swede, tomato, barley and tomato paste. Simmer for 45–50 minutes, or until the vegetables are cooked and the barley is tender. Stir in the parsley and shredded chicken. Simmer until warmed through and season. Serve immediately.

SERVES 4–6

Leek and potato soup

50 g (1¾ oz) butter
1 onion, finely chopped
3 leeks, white part only, sliced
1 celery stalk, finely chopped
1 garlic clove, finely chopped
200 g (7 oz) potatoes, chopped
750 ml (26 fl oz/3 cups) chicken stock
220 ml (7½ fl oz) pouring (whipping) cream
2 tablespoons chopped chives, to garnish

Melt the butter in a large saucepan and add the onion, leek, celery and garlic.
Cover the pan and cook, stirring occasionally, over low heat for 15 minutes, or
until the vegetables are softened but not browned. Add the potato and stock
and bring to the boil.

Reduce the heat and leave to simmer, covered, for 20 minutes. Allow the soup
to cool slightly, then purée in a blender or food processor. Return to the saucepan.

Bring the soup back to the boil and stir in the cream. Season and serve hot or well
chilled, garnished with chives.

SERVES 6

Minestrone

80 g (2¾ oz/½ cup) macaroni
1 tablespoon olive oil
1 leek, sliced
2 garlic cloves, crushed
1 carrot, sliced
1 waxy potato, chopped
1 zucchini (courgette), sliced
2 celery stalks, sliced
100 g (3½ oz) green beans,
    cut into short lengths
425 g (15 oz) tinned chopped
    tomatoes

2 litres (70 fl oz/8 cups)
    vegetable or beef stock
2 tablespoons tomato paste
    (concentrated purée)
425 g (15 oz) tinned cannellini
    beans, rinsed and drained
2 tablespoons chopped flat-leaf
    (Italian) parsley
shaved parmesan cheese,
    to serve

Bring a saucepan of water to the boil. Add the macaroni and cook for about 10–12 minutes, or until *al dente*. Drain and return to the pan to keep warm.

Meanwhile, heat the oil in a large heavy-based saucepan. Add the leek and garlic and cook over medium heat for 3–4 minutes.

Add the carrot, potato, zucchini, celery, green beans, tomato, stock and tomato paste. Bring to the boil, then reduce the heat and simmer for 10 minutes, or until the vegetables are tender.

Stir in the cooked pasta and the cannellini beans and heat through. Garnish with the parsley and shaved parmesan.

SERVES 4

NOTE: Just about any vegetable can be added to minestrone, so this is a great recipe for using up odds and ends.

Caramelised onion and parsnip soup

30 g (1 oz) butter
3 large onions, halved and thinly sliced
2 tablespoons soft brown sugar
250 ml (9 fl oz/1 cup) dry white wine
3 large parsnips, peeled, chopped
1.25 litres (44 fl oz/5 cups) vegetable stock
3 tablespoons pouring (whipping) cream
thyme leaves, to garnish

Melt the butter in a large saucepan. Add the onion and sugar, and cook over low heat for 10 minutes. Add the wine and parsnip, and simmer, covered, for 20 minutes, or until the onion and parsnip are golden and tender.

Pour in the stock, bring to the boil, then reduce the heat and simmer, covered, for 10 minutes. Cool slightly, then place in a blender or food processor and blend in batches until smooth. Season and drizzle with a little cream. Sprinkle the thyme leaves over the top.

SERVES 4

Mushroom soup

40 g (1½ oz) butter
1 onion, finely chopped
12 large (about 1.4 kg/3 lb 3 oz) field mushrooms, finely chopped
2 garlic cloves, crushed
2 tablespoons dry sherry
1 litre (35 fl oz/4 cups) chicken or vegetable stock
2 tablespoons flat-leaf (Italian) parsley, finely chopped
pouring (whipping) cream, to serve

Melt the butter in a large saucepan and fry the onion until the onion is translucent but not browned.

Add the mushroom and garlic and continue frying. The mushrooms might give off a lot of liquid, so fry for 15–20 minutes, or until it is all absorbed back into the mixture.

Add the sherry to the pan, increase the heat and let the mixture bubble—this burns off the alcohol but leaves the flavour. Cool slightly, then transfer to a blender. Process until a smooth paste forms, then add the stock and blend until smooth. Add a couple of tablespoons of cream and blend together. Pour back into the saucepan and heat gently. Garnish with the parsley.

SERVES 4

Gazpacho

1 kg (2 lb 4 oz) vine-ripened tomatoes, chopped
1 Lebanese (short) cucumber, chopped
1 small red capsicum (pepper), seeded and chopped
1 red onion, chopped
3 garlic cloves
80 g (2¾ oz) sourdough bread, crusts removed
2 tablespoons sherry vinegar
Tabasco sauce

Dressing
2 teaspoons each of finely diced tomato, red capsicum (pepper),
    red onion, Lebanese (short) cucumber
2 teaspoons finely chopped flat-leaf (Italian) parsley
1 tablespoon extra virgin olive oil
1 teaspoon lemon juice

Combine the tomatoes, cucumber, capsicum, onion, garlic, sourdough and 250 ml
(9 fl oz/1 cup) of cold water in a blender and blend until smooth. Pass through a
strainer into a bowl, and add the sherry vinegar. Season to taste with salt and
Tabasco, then cover and refrigerate for at least 2 hours, or overnight, to allow the
flavours to develop.

To make the dressing, combine all the ingredients in a small bowl. Season.

Stir the gaspacho well. Spoon the dressing over the top before serving.

SERVES 4

Bouillabaisse

Rouille

1 small red capsicum (pepper)
1 slice of white bread
1 red chilli
2 garlic cloves
1 egg yolk
4 tablespoons olive oil

Soup

2 tablespoons oil
1 fennel bulb, thinly sliced

1 onion, chopped
750 g (1 lb 10 oz) ripe tomatoes
1.25 litres (44 fl oz/5 cups) fish
    stock
pinch of saffron threads
bouquet garni
5 cm (2 inch) piece orange zest
1.5 kg (3 lb 5 oz) monkfish
    fillets, cut into pieces
18 black mussels, cleaned

To make the rouille, cut the capsicum in half, remove the seeds and membrane and place, skin-side up, under the grill (broiler) until the skin blackens. Cool, then peel away the skin. Chop the capsicum flesh. Soak the bread in 3 tablespoons of water, then squeeze dry. Put the capsicum, bread, chilli, garlic and egg yolk in a food processor and process. Add the oil, mixing until smooth. Cover and refrigerate.

Heat the oil in a large saucepan. Cook the fennel and onion for 5 minutes.

Score a cross in the base of each tomato. Cover with boiling water for 30 seconds, then plunge into cold water. Drain and peel the skin. Chop the tomatoes.

Add the tomato to the saucepan and cook for 3 minutes. Stir in the stock, saffron, bouquet garni and orange zest, bring to the boil and boil for 10 minutes. Remove the bouquet garni and orange zest and purée in a blender. Return to the saucepan, season and bring back to the boil. Reduce the heat to a simmer and add the fish and mussels. Cook for 5 minutes, or until the fish is tender and the mussels have opened. Discard any mussels that haven't opened. Serve the soup with rouille.

SERVES 6

Pea and ham soup

500 g (1 lb 2 oz) yellow or green split peas
1½ tablespoons olive oil
2 onions, chopped
1 carrot, diced
3 celery stalks, finely chopped
1 kg (2 lb 8 oz) ham bones or smoked hock, chopped
1 bay leaf
2 thyme sprigs
lemon juice, to taste (optional)

Put the peas in a large bowl, cover with cold water and soak for 6 hours.
Drain well.

Heat the oil in a large saucepan, add the onion, carrot, and celery, and cook over
low heat for 6–7 minutes, or until vegetables are soft.

Add the split peas, ham bones, bay leaf, thyme and 2.5 litres (85 fl oz/10 cups) of
cold water and bring to the boil. Reduce the heat and simmer, stirring occasionally
for 2 hours, or until the peas are tender. Discard the bay leaf and thyme sprigs.

Remove the ham bones from the soup and cool slightly. Remove the meat from
the bone, discard the bones and chop the meat. Return the ham to the soup and
reheat. Season to taste and add lemon juice, if desired.

SERVES 4

Asparagus soup

750 g (1 lb 10 oz) asparagus spears
1 litre (35 fl oz/4 cups) vegetable or chicken stock
30 g (1 oz) butter
1 tablespoon plain (all-purpose) flour
½ teaspoon finely grated lemon zest, plus extra, to garnish

Trim and discard any woody ends from the asparagus spears and cut into 2 cm (¾ inch) lengths. Put in a large saucepan and add 500 ml (17 fl oz/2 cups) of the stock. Cover and bring to the boil, then cook for 10 minutes, or until the asparagus is tender.

Transfer the asparagus and the hot stock to a blender or food processor, and purée in batches until smooth.

Melt the butter in the saucepan over low heat, add the flour, then cook, stirring, for 1 minute, or until pale and foaming. Remove from the heat and gradually add the remaining stock, stirring until smooth after each addition. When all the stock has been added, return the saucepan to the heat, bring to the boil, then simmer for 2 minutes.

Add the asparagus purée to the pan and stir until combined. When heated through, stir in the lemon zest and season. Garnish with the extra lemon zest.

SERVES 4

Borscht

6 large (1.5 kg/3 lb 5 oz) beetroot, peeled
1½ tablespoons caster (superfine) sugar
125 ml (4 fl oz/½ cup) lemon juice
3 eggs
sour cream, to serve (optional)

Grate the beetroot, and put in a saucepan with the caster sugar and 2.25 litres (76 fl oz/9 cups) water. Stir over low heat until the sugar has dissolved. Simmer, partially covered, for about 30 minutes, skimming the surface occasionally.

Add the lemon juice and simmer, uncovered, for 10 minutes. Remove the pan from the heat.

Whisk the eggs in a bowl. Gradually pour the eggs into the beetroot mixture, whisking constantly and taking care not to curdle the eggs. Season to taste. Allow the soup to cool, then cover and refrigerate until cold. Served with a dollop of sour cream, if desired.

SERVES 6

Vegetable soup

105 g (3½ oz/½ cup) dried red kidney beans or borlotti beans
1 tablespoon olive oil
1 leek, halved lengthways and chopped
1 small onion, diced
2 carrots, chopped
2 celery stalks, chopped
1 large zucchini (courgette), chopped
1 tablespoon tomato paste (concentrated purée)
1 litre (35 fl oz/4 cups) vegetable stock
400 g (14 oz) butternut pumpkin (squash),
    cut into 2 cm (¾ inch) cubes
2 potatoes, cut into 2 cm (¾ inch) cubes
3 tablespoons chopped flat-leaf (Italian) parsley

Put the beans in a large bowl, cover with cold water and soak overnight. Rinse, then transfer to a saucepan, cover with cold water and cook for 45 minutes, or until just tender. Drain.

Heat the olive oil in a saucepan. Add the leek and onion and cook over medium heat for 2–3 minutes, without browning, or until they start to soften. Add the carrot, celery and zucchini and cook for 3–4 minutes. Add the tomato paste and stir for 1 minute. Pour in the vegetable stock and 1.25 litres (44 fl oz/5 cups) of water and bring to the boil. Reduce the heat to low and simmer for 20 minutes.

Add the pumpkin, potato, parsley and beans and simmer for a further 20 minutes, or until the vegetables are tender and the beans are cooked. Season well.

SERVES 6

Cabbage soup

100 g (3½ oz/½ cup) dried haricot beans
125 g (4½ oz) bacon, cubed
40 g (1½ oz) butter
1 carrot, sliced
1 onion, chopped
1 leek, white part only, roughly chopped
1 turnip, peeled and chopped
bouquet garni
1.25 litres (44 fl oz/5 cups) chicken stock
400 g (14 oz) white cabbage, finely shredded

Soak the beans overnight in cold water. Drain, put in a saucepan and cover with cold water. Bring to the boil and simmer for 5 minutes, then drain. Put the bacon in the same saucepan, cover with water and simmer for 5 minutes. Drain and pat dry with paper towels.

Melt the butter in a large heavy-based saucepan. Add the bacon and cook for 5 minutes, without browning. Add the beans, carrot, onion, leek and turnip and cook for 5 minutes. Add the bouquet garni and chicken stock and bring to the boil. Cover and simmer for 30 minutes. Add the cabbage, uncover and simmer for 30 minutes, or until the beans are tender. Remove the bouquet garni before serving and season to taste.

SERVES 4

hot

Sweet potato and chilli soup

1 tablespoon oil
1 onion, chopped
2 garlic cloves, finely chopped
1–2 small red chillies, finely chopped
¼ teaspoon paprika
750 g (1 lb 10 oz) orange sweet potato, chopped into small pieces
1 litre (35 fl oz/4 cups) vegetable or beef stock
chopped dried chilli, to garnish

Heat the oil in a large heavy-based saucepan. Add the onion and cook for about 1–2 minutes, or until soft. Add the garlic, chilli and paprika and cook for a further 2 minutes, or until aromatic. Add the sweet potato to the pan and toss to coat with the spices.

Pour in the stock and bring to the boil. Reduce the heat and simmer for 15 minutes, or until the vegetables are tender. Cool slightly, then transfer to a blender or food processor and blend in batches until smooth, adding extra water if needed to reach the desired consistency.

Season to taste and sprinkle with dried chilli before serving.

SERVES 4

Laksa

200 g (7 oz) dried rice vermicelli
2 tablespoons peanut oil
2–3 tablespoons laksa paste
1 litre (35 fl oz/4 cups) vegetable stock
750 ml (26 fl oz/3 cups) coconut milk
250 g (9 oz) snow peas (mangetout), halved diagonally
5 spring onions (scallions), cut into 3 cm (1¼ inch) lengths
2 tablespoons lime juice
125 g (4½ oz) bean sprouts, trimmed
200 g (7 oz) fried tofu puffs, halved
3 tablespoons roughly chopped Vietnamese mint
20 g (¾ oz) coriander (cilantro) leaves

Put the vermicelli in a large bowl, cover with boiling water and soak for 5 minutes.

Heat the oil in a large saucepan, add the laksa paste and cook, stirring, over medium heat for 1 minute, or until fragrant. Add the stock, coconut milk, snow peas and spring onion and simmer for 5 minutes. Pour in the lime juice and season to taste.

Drain the vermicelli and add the bean sprouts and fried tofu puffs. Ladle the hot soup over the vermicelli. Serve immediately, sprinkled with the mint and coriander.

SERVES 4

Curried chicken noodle soup

- 175 g (6 oz) dried thin egg noodles
- 2 tablespoons peanut oil
- 2 boneless, skinless chicken breasts (250 g/9 oz each)
- 1 onion, sliced
- 1 small fresh red chilli, seeded and finely chopped
- 1 tablespoon finely chopped fresh ginger
- 2 tablespoons Indian curry powder
- 750 ml (26 fl oz/3 cups) chicken stock
- 800 ml (28 fl oz) coconut milk
- 300 g (10½ oz) baby bok choy, cut into long strips
- 20 g (¾ oz) basil, torn

Cook the noodles in a large saucepan of boiling water for 3–4 minutes, or until soft. Drain well and set aside.

Heat the oil in a large saucepan and add the chicken. Cook on each side for 5 minutes, or until cooked through. Remove the chicken and keep warm.

Put the onion in the pan and cook over low heat for 8 minutes, or until softened but not browned. Add the chilli, ginger and curry powder and cook for a further 2 minutes. Add the chicken stock and bring to the boil. Reduce the heat and simmer for 20 minutes. Thinly slice the chicken on the diagonal.

Add the coconut milk to the saucepan and simmer for 10 minutes. Add the bok choy and cook for 3 minutes, then stir in the basil.

To serve, divide the noodles among four deep serving bowls. Top with slices of chicken and ladle in the soup. Serve immediately.

SERVES 4

Caribbean fish soup

2 tomatoes
2 tablespoons oil
4 French shallots, finely chopped
2 celery stalks, chopped
1 large red capsicum (pepper), chopped
1 Scotch bonnet chilli, deseeded and finely chopped (see Note)
½ teaspoon ground allspice
½ teaspoon freshly grated nutmeg

850 ml (30 fl oz) fish stock
275 g (9¾ oz) orange sweet potato, peeled and cut into cubes
3 tablespoons lime juice
500 g (1 lb 2 oz) skinless sea bream fillets, cut into chunks

Fish substitution
sea bass, cod

Score a cross in the base of each tomato. Soak in boiling water for 30 seconds, then plunge into cold water. Drain and peel the skin away from the cross. Chop the tomatoes, discarding the cores, and reserving any juices.

Heat the oil in a large saucepan, then add the shallots, celery, capsicum, chilli, allspice and nutmeg. Cook for 4–5 minutes, or until the vegetables have softened, stirring occasionally. Tip in the chopped tomatoes (including their juices) and stock and bring to the boil. Reduce the heat to medium and add the cubes of sweet potato. Season to taste and cook for about 15 minutes, or until the sweet potato is tender.

Add the lime juice and chunks of fish to the saucepan and poach gently for 4–5 minutes, or until the fish is cooked through. Season to taste.

SERVES 6

NOTE: Scotch bonnet chillies looks like a mini capsicum (pepper) and can be green, red or orange. They are extremely hot but have a good, slightly acidic flavour.

Chicken and galangal soup

5 cm x 2 cm (2 in x ¾ in) piece fresh galangal, peeled and
    cut into thin slices
500 ml (17 fl oz/2 cups) coconut milk
250 ml (9 fl oz/1 cup) chicken stock
4 makrut (kaffir lime) leaves, torn
1 tablespoon finely chopped coriander (cilantro) roots
500 g (1 lb 2 oz) chicken breast fillets, cut into thin strips
1–2 teaspoons finely chopped fresh red chillies
2 tablespoons fish sauce
1½ tablespoons lime juice
3 teaspoons palm sugar or soft brown sugar
1 small handful coriander (cilantro) leaves, chopped

Place the galangal in a saucepan with the coconut milk, stock, lime leaves and coriander roots. Bring to the boil, reduce the heat to low and simmer for 10 minutes, stirring occasionally.

Add the chicken and chilli to the pan and simmer for 8 minutes.

Stir in the fish sauce, lime juice and palm sugar and cook for 1 minute. Stir in the coriander leaves. Serve immediately garnished with extra coriander, if desired.

SERVES 4

Beef pho

200 g (7 oz) rice noodle sticks
1.5 litres (52 fl oz/6 cups) beef
   stock
1 star anise
4 cm (1½ inch) piece fresh
   ginger, sliced
2 pigs trotters
½ onion, studded with 2 cloves
2 stems lemon grass, pounded
2 garlic cloves, pounded
¼ teaspoon white pepper
1 tablespoon fish sauce
400 g (14 oz) beef fillet,
   partially frozen, and
   thinly sliced

90 g (3¼ oz/1 cup) bean sprouts
2 spring onions (scallions),
   thinly sliced on the diagonal
25 g (1 oz) coriander (cilantro)
   leaves, chopped
25 g (1 oz) Vietnamese mint,
   chopped
1 fresh red chilli, thinly sliced
fresh red chillies, extra, to serve
Vietnamese mint, extra,
   to serve
coriander (cilantro) leaves,
   extra, to serve
2 limes, cut into quarters
fish sauce, extra, to serve

Soak the noodles in boiling water for 15–20 minutes. Drain.

Bring the stock, star anise, ginger, trotters, onion, lemon grass, garlic and white pepper to the boil in a large saucepan. Reduce the heat and simmer for 30 minutes. Strain, return to the same pan and stir in the fish sauce.

Divide the noodles among bowls, then top with beef strips, sprouts, spring onion, coriander, mint and chilli. Ladle on the broth.

Pute the extra chilli, mint, coriander, lime quarters and fish sauce in small bowls on a platter and serve with the soup.

SERVES 4

Mexican soup with salsa

3 tablespoons olive oil
1 large onion, chopped
1 large celery stalk, chopped
3 garlic cloves, crushed
2 thin red chillies, chopped
200 ml (7 fl oz) fish stock
800 g (1 lb 12 oz) tinned
    chopped tomatoes
2 bay leaves
1 teaspoon dried oregano
1 teaspoon caster (superfine)
    sugar
2 corn cobs, kernels removed
500 g (1 lb 2 oz) halibut fillets

2 tablespoons chopped
    coriander (cilantro) leaves
juice of 2 limes
12 prawns (shrimp), tails intact
8 scallops, cleaned
12 clams, cleaned
125 g (4½ oz/½ cup) thick
    (double/heavy) cream

Salsa
½ small avocado
1 tablespoon coriander
    (cilantro) leaves
grated zest and juice of 1 lime
½ red onion, finely chopped

Heat the oil in a saucepan. Add the onion and celery and cook over medium heat for 10 minutes. Add the garlic and chilli and cook for 1 minute, stirring. Add the fish stock and tomatoes. Stir in the bay leaves, oregano and sugar and bring to the boil. Reduce the heat to low and simmer for 10 minutes. Remove the bay leaves, then tip the tomato mixture into a food processor and whiz until smooth. Return the tomato sauce to the pan and season. Add the corn kernels and bring back to the boil. Reduce the heat and simmer for 3 minutes. Cut the fish into chunks. Stir the coriander and the lime juice into the sauce, add the fish to the pan, then simmer for 1 minute. Add the prawns, scallops and clams. Cover with a lid and cook for a further 2–3 minutes, or until the seafood is cooked through.

To make the salsa, chop the avocado into cubes and mix with the coriander, the lime zest and juice, and red onion. Stir the cream into the soup and top with salsa.

SERVES 4

Thai spicy sour soup

750 ml (26 fl oz/3 cups) vegetable stock
2 tablespoons Tom Yum paste (see Note)
2 cm x 2 cm (¾ inch x ¾ inch) piece galangal,
    peeled and cut into thin slices
1 lemon grass stem, lightly crushed and cut into 4 lengths
3 makrut (kaffir lime) leaves
1 small red chilli, finely sliced on the diagonal (optional)
200 g (7 oz) button mushrooms, halved
200 g (7 oz) silken firm tofu, cut into 1.5 cm (⅝ inch) cubes
200 g (7 oz) baby bok choy (pak choi), roughly shredded
2 tablespoons lime juice
1 small handful coriander (cilantro) leaves

Place the stock, Tom Yum paste, galangal, lemon grass, kaffir lime leaves, chilli and 750 ml (26 fl oz/3 cups) of water in a saucepan. Cover and bring to the boil, then reduce the heat and simmer for 5 minutes.

Add the mushrooms and tofu and simmer for 5 minutes, or until the mushrooms are tender. Add the bok choy and simmer for a further minute, or until wilted. Remove the pan from the heat and stir in the lime juice and coriander leaves before serving.

SERVES 4–6

NOTE: For vegetarian cooking, make sure you buy a brand of Tom Yum paste that does not contain shrimp paste or fish sauce.

Chicken and pumpkin laksa

Paste
2 bird's eye chillies, chopped
2 lemon grass stems, white part
   only, chopped
4 red Asian shallots, peeled
1 tablespoon chopped ginger
1 teaspoon ground turmeric
3 candlenuts (optional)

110 g (3¾ oz) dried rice noodle
   sticks
1 tablespoon peanut oil

250 g (9 oz) butternut pumpkin
   (squash), cut into chunks
800 ml (28 fl oz) coconut milk
600 g (1 lb 5 oz) chicken breast
   fillets, cut into cubes
2 tablespoons lime juice
1 tablespoon fish sauce
90 g (3¼ oz) bean sprouts
15 g (½ oz) torn basil
10 g (¼ oz) torn mint
50 g (1¾ oz/½ cup) unsalted
   peanuts, toasted and chopped
1 lime, cut into quarters

Put all the paste ingredients in a food processor with 1 tablespoon of water and blend until smooth.

Soak the noodles in boiling water for 15–20 minutes. Drain.

Meanwhile, heat the oil in a wok and swirl to coat. Add the paste and stir over low heat for 5 minutes, or until aromatic. Add the pumpkin and coconut milk and simmer for 10 minutes. Add the chicken and simmer for 20 minutes. Stir in the lime juice and fish sauce.

Divide the noodles among four deep serving bowls, then ladle the soup over them. Top with the bean sprouts, basil, mint, peanuts and lime.

SERVES 4

Curried lentil, carrot and cashew soup

1.5 litres (52 fl oz/6 cups) vegetable or chicken stock
750 g (1 lb 10 oz) carrots, grated
185 g (6½ oz/¾ cup) red lentils, rinsed and drained
1 tablespoon olive oil
1 large onion, chopped
80 g (2¾ oz/½ cup) unsalted cashew nuts
1 tablespoon Madras curry paste
25 g (1 oz) chopped coriander (cilantro) leaves and stems
125 g (4½ oz/½ cup) Greek-style yoghurt
coriander (cilantro) leaves, to garnish

Bring the stock to the boil in a large saucepan. Add the carrots and lentils, bring the mixture back to the boil. Simmer over low heat for about 8 minutes, or until the carrot and lentils are soft.

Meanwhile, heat the oil in a large frying pan. Add the onion and cashews and cook over medium heat for 2–3 minutes, or until the onion is soft and browned. Add the curry paste and coriander and cook for a further 1 minute, or until fragrant. Stir the paste into the carrot and lentil mixture.

Transfer to a food processor or blender and process in batches until smooth. Return the mixture to the pan and reheat over medium heat until hot. Season to taste and serve with a dollop of yoghurt and a sprinkling of coriander.

SERVES 6

NOTE: Garnish the soup with a pinch of chilli flakes to give it an extra kick.

Vietnamese beef soup

400 g (14 oz) rump steak, trimmed
½ onion
1½ tablespoons fish sauce
1 star anise
1 cinnamon stick
pinch ground white pepper
1.5 litres (52 fl oz/6 cups) beef stock
300 g (10½ oz) fresh thin rice noodles
3 spring onions (scallions), thinly sliced
15 g (½ oz) Vietnamese mint leaves
90 g (3¼ oz/1 cup) bean sprouts
1 small white onion, cut in half and thinly sliced
1 small red chilli, thinly sliced on the diagonal
lemon wedges, to serve

Wrap the rump steak in plastic wrap and freeze for 40 minutes.

Meanwhile, put the onion, fish sauce, star anise, cinnamon stick, pepper, stock and 500 ml (17 fl oz/2 cups) water in a large saucepan. Bring to the boil, then reduce the heat, cover and simmer for 20 minutes. Discard the onion, star anise and cinnamon stick.

Cover the noodles with boiling water and gently separate the strands. Drain and refresh under cold water.

Remove the meat from the freezer and thinly slice it across the grain.

Divide the noodles and spring onion among four deep bowls. Top with the beef, mint, bean sprouts, onion and chilli. Ladle the hot broth over the top and serve with the lemon wedges.

SERVES 4

NOTE: In Vietnam, noodle soups are called pho — beef noodle soup, pho bo, is one of the most popular.

Pumpkin and red lentil soup

1 tablespoon olive oil
1 long red chilli, seeded and chopped
1 onion, finely chopped
500 g (1 lb 2 oz) butternut pumpkin (squash), chopped
350 g (12 oz) orange sweet potato, chopped
1.5 litres (52 fl oz/6 cups) vegetable stock
125 g (4½ oz/½ cup) red lentils
1 tablespoon tahini
red chilli, extra, to garnish

Heat the oil in a large saucepan over medium heat. Add the chilli and onion and cook for 2–3 minutes, or until the onion is soft. Reduce the heat to low, add the pumpkin and sweet potato and cook, covered, for 8 minutes, stirring occasionally.

Increase the heat to high, add the stock and bring to the boil. Reduce the heat to low, and simmer, covered, for 10 minutes. Add the red lentils and cook, covered, for 7 minutes, or until tender.

Process the soup in batches in a blender or food processor. Add the tahini and blend until smooth. Return to the saucepan and gently heat until warmed through. Garnish with chilli.

SERVES 4

Rice noodle soup with duck

1 whole Chinese roast duck
4 coriander (cilantro) roots and
   stems, well rinsed
5 slices fresh galangal
4 spring onions (scallions), sliced
   on the diagonal into 3 cm
   (1¼ inch) lengths
400 g (14 oz) Chinese broccoli,
   cut into 5 cm (2 inch) lengths
2 garlic cloves, crushed
3 tablespoons fish sauce
1 tablespoon hoisin sauce
2 teaspoons grated palm sugar
   or soft brown sugar
½ teaspoon ground white
   pepper
500 g (1 lb 2 oz) fresh rice
   noodles
crispy fried garlic flakes,
   to garnish (optional)
coriander (cilantro) leaves,
   to garnish (optional)

To make the stock, cut off the duck's head and discard. Remove the skin and fat, leaving the neck intact. Remove the flesh from the bones and set aside. Cut any fat from the carcass along with the parson's nose, then discard. Break the carcass into pieces, then put in a stockpot with 2 litres (70 fl oz/8 cups) of water.

Bruise the coriander roots and stems with the back of a knife. Add to the pot with the galangal and bring to the boil. Skim off any foam from the surface. Boil over medium heat for 15 minutes. Strain the stock through a fine sieve, discard the carcass, and return the stock to a clean saucepan.

Slice the duck flesh into strips. Add to the stock with the spring onion, Chinese broccoli, garlic, fish sauce, hoisin sauce, palm sugar and white pepper. Gently bring to the boil.

Cook the noodles in boiling water for 2–3 minutes, or until tender. Drain well. Divide the noodles and soup evenly among the serving bowls. If desired, garnish with the garlic flakes and coriander leaves.

SERVES 4–6

Hot and sour
prawn soup

350 g (12 oz) raw medium
    prawns (shrimp)
1 tablespoon oil
3 lemon grass stems, white part
    only
3 thin slices fresh galangal
3–5 small fresh red chillies
5 makrut (kaffir lime) leaves,
    finely shredded
2 tablespoons fish sauce

2 spring onions (scallions), sliced
70 g (2½ oz/½ cup) canned
    straw mushrooms, drained,
    or quartered button
    mushrooms
3 tablespoons lime juice
1–2 tablespoons chilli paste, or
    to taste
coriander (cilantro) leaves,
    to garnish (optional)

Peel and devein the prawns, leaving the tail intact and reserving the heads and shells.

Heat the oil in a large stockpot or wok and add the prawn heads and shells. Cook for 5 minutes, or until the shells turn bright orange. Bruise 1 stem of the lemon grass with the back of a knife. Add to the pan with the galangal and 2 litres (70 fl oz/ 8 cups) water. Bring to the boil, then reduce the heat and simmer for 20 minutes. Strain the stock and return to the pan. Discard the shells and herbs.

Finely slice the chillies and remaining lemon grass. Add to the liquid with the lime leaves, fish sauce, spring onion and mushrooms. Cook gently for 2 minutes.

Add the prawns and cook for 3 minutes, or until the prawns are tender. Add the lime juice and chilli paste (adjust to taste with extra lime juice or fish sauce). If desired, garnish with coriander leaves.

SERVES 4–6

Green curry
vegetable soup

2 teaspoons peanut oil
1 tablespoon green curry paste
3 makrut (kaffir lime) leaves
1.25 litres (44 fl oz/5 cups) vegetable or chicken stock
670 ml (23 fl oz/2⅔ cups) coconut milk
600 g (1 lb 5 oz) butternut pumpkin (squash),
    cut into 1.5 cm (⅝ inch) cubes
250 g (9 oz) small yellow squash (pattypan squash), sliced
115 g (4 oz) fresh baby corn spears, halved lengthways
2 tablespoons mushroom soy sauce
2 tablespoons lime juice
1 teaspoon sugar
1½ tablespoons Vietnamese mint, finely chopped

Heat the oil in a large saucepan and add the curry paste and lime leaves. Cook, stirring, over medium heat for 1 minute, or until fragrant.

Bring the stock to the boil in a separate saucepan.

Gradually add the stock and coconut milk to the curry mixture and bring to the boil. Add the pumpkin, squash and corn, and simmer over low heat for 12 minutes, or until the pumpkin is tender.

Add the soy sauce and lime juice, and season to taste with sugar, salt and black pepper. Garnish with the mint before serving.

SERVES 6

Beef and chilli bean soup

1 tablespoon oil
1 red onion, finely chopped
2 garlic cloves, crushed
2½ teaspoons chilli flakes
2½ teaspoons ground cumin
2½ tablespoons finely chopped coriander (cilantro) root and stem
1½ teaspoons ground coriander
500 g (1 lb 2 oz) lean minced (ground) beef
1 tablespoon tomato paste (concentrated purée)
4 tomatoes, peeled, seeded and diced
420 g (15 oz) tinned red kidney beans, drained and rinsed
2 litres (70 fl oz/8 cups) beef stock
3 tablespoons chopped coriander (cilantro) leaves
80 g (2¾ oz/⅓ cup) sour cream

Heat the oil in a large saucepan over medium heat. Cook the onion for about
2–3 minutes, or until softened. Add the garlic, chilli flakes, cumin, fresh and
ground coriander, and cook for 1 minute. Add the beef and cook for 3–4 minutes,
or until cooked through — break up any lumps with a spoon.

Add the tomato paste, tomato, beans and stock and bring to the boil. Reduce the
heat and simmer for 15–20 minutes, or until reduced slightly. Remove any scum
on the surface. Stir in the chopped coriander. Serve with sour cream.

SERVES 4

Gumbo

Roux
4 tablespoons oil
75 g (2½ oz/⅔ cup) plain
    (all-purpose) flour
1 onion, finely chopped

4 crabs, cleaned
450 g (1 lb) chorizo sausage
6 spring onions (scallions), sliced
1 green capsicum (pepper),
    roughly chopped

3 tablespoons chopped flat-leaf
    (Italian) parsley
¼ teaspoon chilli powder
500 g (1 lb 2 oz) prawns (shrimp),
    peeled and deveined
24 oysters, shucked
½ teaspoon filé powder (see
    Note)
1½ tablespoons long-grain rice

To make the roux, pour the oil into a heavy-based saucepan over low heat. Add the flour, stirring after each addition, to make a thin roux. Continue to stir over low heat for 35 minutes, or until dark brown. Add the onion and cook for 4 minutes, or until tender. Pour in 1.5 litres (52 fl oz/6 cups) of boiling water, stirring to dissolve the roux, and bring to a simmer.

Cut the crabs into pieces. Cut the chorizo into pieces. Add the crab, sausage, spring onion, capsicum, parsley and chilli powder to the roux. Cook for about 30 minutes, then add the prawns and the oysters and their juices and cook for a further 5 minutes, or until the prawns are pink. Season, then stir in the filé powder.

Meanwhile, cook the rice in salted boiling water for about 10 minutes, or until just cooked through. Put a couple of tablespoons of rice in the bottom of each bowl and ladle over the gumbo. Serve immediately.

SERVES 6

NOTE: Filé powder is a flavouring often used in Creole cooking. It is made by drying, then grinding sassafras leaves.

Tom yum goong

1 tablespoon oil
500 g (1 lb 2 oz) prawns
   (shrimp), peeled and
   deveined, reserving the
   heads and shells
2 tablespoons Thai red curry
   paste or tom yum paste
2 tablespoons tamarind purée
   (see Note)
2 teaspoons ground turmeric

1 teaspoon chopped red chillies
4 makrut (kaffir lime) leaves,
   shredded
2 tablespoons fish sauce
2 tablespoons lime juice
2 teaspoons grated palm sugar
   or soft brown sugar
2 tablespoons coriander
   (cilantro) leaves

Heat the oil in a large saucepan or wok and cook the prawn heads and shells for 10 minutes over medium heat, stirring frequently, until the heads are deep orange in colour.

Add 250 ml (9 fl oz/1 cup) of water and the curry paste to the saucepan. Bring to the boil and cook for 5 minutes, or until reduced slightly. Add another 2 litres (70 fl oz/8 cups) of water and simmer for 20 minutes. Strain, discarding the shells and heads, and pour the stock back into the pan.

Add the tamarind, turmeric, chillies and lime leaves to the saucepan. Bring to the boil and cook for 2 minutes. Add the prawns and cook for 5 minutes, or until pink. Stir in the fish sauce, lime juice and sugar. Serve sprinkled with coriander leaves.

SERVES 4–6

NOTE: If you are unable to find tamarind purée, you can make your own by soaking a 225 g (8 oz) packet of tamarind pulp in 500 ml (17 fl oz/2 cups) of boiling water for 1–2 hours, crushing occasionally. Push through a sieve and discard the fibres. Alternatively, use lemon juice.

Chilli, corn and red capsicum soup

1 coriander (cilantro) sprig
4 sweet corn cobs
30 g (1 oz) butter
2 red capsicums (peppers), diced
1 small onion, finely chopped
1 small red chilli, finely chopped
1 tablespoon plain (all-purpose) flour
500 ml (17 fl oz/2 cups) vegetable stock
125 ml (4 fl oz/½ cup) pouring (whipping) cream

Trim the leaves off the coriander and finely chop the root and stems. Cut the kernels off the corn cobs.

Heat the butter in a saucepan over medium heat. Add the corn kernels, capsicum, onion and chilli and stir to coat in the butter. Cook, covered, over low heat, stirring occasionally, for 10 minutes, or until soft. Increase the heat to medium, add the coriander root and stem and cook, stirring, for 30 seconds, or until fragrant. Sprinkle with the flour and stir for 1 minute. Remove from the heat and gradually stir in the stock. Add 500 ml (17 fl oz/2 cups) of water and return to the heat. Bring to the boil, reduce the heat to low and simmer, covered, for 30 minutes, or until the vegetables are tender. Cool slightly.

Pour 500 ml (17 fl oz/2 cups) of the soup into a blender and purée until smooth. Return the purée to the soup in the pan, pour in the cream and gently heat until warmed through. Season. Sprinkle with the coriander leaves.

SERVES 4

creamy

Zucchini pesto soup

1 tablespoon olive oil
1 large onion, finely chopped
2 garlic cloves, crushed
750 ml (26 fl oz/3 cups)
    vegetable or chicken stock
750 g (1 lb 10 oz) zucchini
    (courgettes), thinly sliced
3 tablespoons pouring
    (whipping) cream
toasted ciabatta bread, to serve

Pesto
50 g (1¾ oz/1 cup) basil
25 g (1 oz/¼ cup) finely grated
    parmesan cheese
2 tablespoons pine nuts,
    toasted
2 tablespoons extra virgin
    olive oil

Heat the oil in a large heavy-based saucepan. Add the onion and garlic and cook over medium heat for 5 minutes, or until the onion is soft.

Bring the stock to the boil in a separate saucepan. Add the zucchini and hot stock to the onion mixture. Bring to the boil, then reduce the heat. Cover and simmer for 10 minutes, or until the zucchini is very soft.

To make the pesto, process the basil, parmesan and pine nuts in a food processor for 20 seconds, or until finely chopped. Gradually add the olive oil and process until smooth. Spoon into a small bowl.

Transfer the zucchini mixture to a blender or food processor and blend in batches until smooth. Return the mixture to the pan, stir in the cream and 2 tablespoons of the pesto, and reheat over medium heat until hot. Season and serve with toasted ciabatta bread.

SERVES 4

Orange sweet potato soup

40 g (1½ oz) butter
2 onions, chopped
2 garlic cloves, crushed
1 kg (2 lb 4 oz) orange sweet potato, peeled and chopped
1 large celery stalk, chopped
1 large green apple, peeled, cored and chopped
1½ teaspoons ground cumin
2 litres (70 fl oz/8 cups) chicken stock
125 g (4½ oz/½ cup) natural yoghurt
lavash bread, to serve (optional)

Melt the butter in a large saucepan over low heat. Add the onion and cook, stirring occasionally, for 10 minutes, or until soft. Add the garlic, sweet potato, celery, apple and 1 teaspoon of the cumin and cook for 5–7 minutes, or until well coated. Add the chicken stock and the remaining cumin and bring to the boil over high heat. Reduce the heat and simmer for 25–30 minutes, or until the sweet potato is very soft.

Cool the soup slightly and blend in batches until smooth. Return to the pan and gently stir over medium heat until warmed through. Season and serve with a dollop of yoghurt and toasted lavash bread, if desired.

SERVES 4–6

Prawn, potato and corn chowder

600 g (lb 5 oz) raw prawns (shrimp)
3 corn cobs, husks removed
1 tablespoon olive oil
2 leeks, white part only, finely chopped
2 garlic cloves, crushed
650 g (1 lb 7 oz) potatoes, cut into 1.5 cm (⅝ inch) cubes

750 ml (26 fl oz/3 cups) fish or chicken stock
375 ml (13 fl oz/1½ cups) milk
250 ml (9 fl oz/1 cup) pouring (whipping) cream
pinch of cayenne pepper
3 tablespoons finely chopped flat-leaf (Italian) parsley

Peel and devein the prawns, then chop into 1.5 cm (⅝ inch) pieces. Cut the kernels from the corn cobs.

Heat the oil in a large saucepan and add the leek. Cook over medium–low heat for about 5 minutes, or until soft and lightly golden. Add the garlic and cook for 30 seconds, then add the corn, potato, stock and milk.

Bring to the boil, then reduce the heat. Simmer, partially covered, for 20 minutes, or until the potato is soft but still holds its shape. Remove the lid and simmer for a further 10 minutes to allow the soup to thicken. Reduce the heat to low. Put 500 ml (17 fl oz/2 cups) of the soup in a blender and blend until very smooth.

Return the blended soup to the saucepan and add the prawns. Increase the heat to medium and simmer for 2 minutes, or until the prawns are pink and cooked through. Stir in the cream, cayenne pepper and 2 tablespoons of the parsley. Season to taste, then serve garnished with the remaining parsley.

SERVES 4–6

Fresh mushroom,
shallot and sour cream soup

40 g (1½ oz) butter
100 g (3½ oz) French shallots, roughly chopped
3 garlic cloves, crushed
30 g (1 oz) flat-leaf (Italian) parsley
315 ml (10¾ fl oz/1¼ cups) vegetable or chicken stock
315 ml (10¾ fl oz/1¼ cups) milk
600 g (1 lb 5 oz) button mushrooms, chopped,
    plus extra to garnish (optional)
¼ teaspoon ground nutmeg
¼ teaspoon cayenne pepper, plus extra to garnish
150 g (5½ oz) light sour cream

Melt the butter in a large heavy-based saucepan and add the shallots, garlic and parsley. Cook over medium heat for 2–3 minutes.

Put the stock and milk in a separate saucepan and bring to the boil.

Add the mushrooms to the shallot mixture. Season, then stir in the nutmeg and cayenne pepper. Cook, stirring, for 1 minute. Add the stock and milk, bring to the boil, then reduce the heat and simmer for 5 minutes. Transfer the soup to a blender or food processor and blend until smooth. Return to the pan.

Stir in the sour cream and reheat gently. Season to taste and serve sprinkled with cayenne pepper. Garnish with the extra mushrooms, lightly fried in butter, if desired.

SERVES 4

Watercress soup

30 g (1 oz) butter
1 onion, finely chopped
250 g (9 oz) potatoes, diced
625 ml (21½ fl oz/2½ cups) chicken stock
1 kg (2 lb 4 oz) watercress, trimmed and chopped
125 ml (4 fl oz/½ cup) pouring (whipping) cream
125 ml (4 fl oz/½ cup) milk
freshly grated nutmeg
2 tablespoons chopped chives

Melt the butter in a large saucepan and add the onion. Cover the pan and cook over low heat until the onion is softened. Add the potato and chicken stock and simmer for 12 minutes, or until the potato is tender. Add the watercress and cook for 1 minute.

Remove from the heat and leave the soup to cool a little. Pour into a blender or food processor and blend until smooth. Return to the saucepan.

Bring the soup gently back to the boil and stir in the cream and milk. Season with nutmeg, salt and pepper and reheat without boiling. Serve garnished with chives.

SERVES 4

Creamy chicken and corn soup

20 g (¾ oz) butter
1 tablespoon olive oil
500 g (1 lb 2 oz) chicken thigh
   fillets, trimmed and
   thinly sliced
2 garlic cloves, chopped
1 leek, chopped
1 large celery stalk, chopped
1 bay leaf
½ teaspoon thyme

1 litre (35 fl oz/4 cups) chicken
   stock
3 tablespoons sherry
550 g (1 lb 4 oz) corn kernels
   (fresh, canned or frozen)
1 large floury potato (russet),
   cut into 1 cm (½ inch) cubes
185 ml (6 fl oz/¾ cup) pouring
   (whipping) cream
chives, to garnish

Melt the butter and oil in a large saucepan over high heat. Cook the chicken in batches for 3 minutes, or until lightly golden and just cooked through. Place in a bowl, cover and refrigerate until needed.

Reduce the heat to medium and stir in the garlic, leek, celery, bay leaf and thyme. Cook for 2 minutes, or until the leek softens. Add the stock, sherry and 500 ml (17 fl oz/2 cups) of water and stir to combine. Add the corn and potato and bring to the boil. Reduce the heat and simmer for 1 hour, skimming any scum off the surface. Cool slightly.

Remove the bay leaf and purée the soup in a blender or food processor. Return to the pan and add the cream and chicken. Stir over medium heat for 2–3 minutes, or until heated through. Season. Serve with extra cream and garnish with chives.

SERVES 4–6

Corn and lemon grass soup with yabbies

4 corn cobs
1 tablespoon oil
1 leek, white part only, chopped
1 celery stick, chopped
3 lemon grass stems, white part only, bruised
5 garlic cloves, crushed
1 teaspoon ground cumin
1 teaspoon ground coriander
¾ teaspoon ground white pepper
3 makrut (kaffir lime) leaves

750 ml (26 fl oz/3 cups) chicken stock
800 ml (28 fl oz) coconut milk
125 ml (4 fl oz/½ cup) pouring (whipping) cream
2 teaspoons butter
½ teaspoon sambal oelek
1.2 kg (2 lb 12 oz) cooked yabbies or crayfish, shredded
1 tablespoon finely chopped coriander (cilantro) leaves

Trim the kernels from the corn. Heat the oil in a saucepan over medium heat. Add the leek, celery and lemon grass. Stir for 10 minutes, or until the leek is soft. Add half the garlic, and the cumin, coriander and ½ teaspoon of the pepper. Cook, stirring, for 1–2 minutes, or until fragrant. Add the corn, lime leaves, stock and coconut milk, stir well and simmer, for 1½ hours. Remove from the heat and cool. Remove the lemon grass and lime leaves and blend the mixture in batches in a food processor.

Push the mixture through a sieve. Repeat. Return to a saucepan, add the cream and warm gently.

Melt the butter in a frying pan over medium heat, add the remaining garlic, sambal oelek, remaining pepper and a pinch of salt and stir for 1 minute. Add the yabby meat, stir for a further minute, then remove from the heat and stir in the coriander.

SERVES 4

Cauliflower and almond soup with hot cheese rolls

75 g (2½ oz/½ cup) blanched
   almonds
1 tablespoon olive oil
1 leek, white part only, chopped
2 garlic cloves, crushed
1 kg (2 lb 4 oz) cauliflower, cut
   into small florets
2 desiree potatoes, cut into
   1.5 cm (⅝ in) pieces
1.75 litres (60 fl oz/7 cups)
   chicken stock

Cheese rolls
4 round bread rolls
40 g (1½ oz) softened butter
125 g (4½ oz) cheddar cheese,
   grated
50 g (1¾ oz) parmesan cheese,
   grated

Preheat the oven to 180°C (350°F/Gas 4). Put the almonds on a baking tray and toast for 5 minutes, or until golden.

Heat the oil in a large saucepan over medium heat and cook the leek for 2–3 minutes, or until softened. Add the garlic and cook for 30 seconds, then add the cauliflower, potato and stock. Bring to the boil, then reduce the heat and simmer for 15 minutes, or until the vegetables are very tender. Cool for 5 minutes.

Blend the soup with the almonds in batches in a blender until smooth. Season to taste. Return to the pan and stir over medium heat until heated through. Serve with the cheese rolls, if desired.

To make the cheese rolls, split the rolls and butter both sides. Combine the grated cheeses and divide evenly among the rolls. Sandwich together and wrap in foil. Bake in the oven for 15–20 minutes, or until the cheese has melted.

SERVES 4

Potato and sweet corn chowder

6 sweet corn cobs
2 tablespoons vegetable oil
1 onion, finely diced
3 garlic cloves, crushed
1 celery stalk, diced
1 carrot, peeled and diced
2 large potatoes, peeled and diced
1 litre (35 fl oz/4 cups) vegetable or chicken stock
2 tablespoons finely chopped flat-leaf (Italian) parsley

Bring a large saucepan of salted water to the boil. Cook the sweet corn for 5 minutes. Reserve 250 ml (9 fl oz/1 cup) of the cooking water. Cut the corn kernels from the cob, place half in a blender with the reserved cooking water, and blend until smooth.

Heat the oil in a large saucepan. Add the onion, garlic, celery and a large pinch of salt and cook for 5 minutes. Add the carrot and potatoes, cook for a further 5 minutes, then add the stock, corn kernels and blended corn mixture. Reduce the heat and simmer for 20 minutes, or until the vegetables are tender. Season well and stir in the chopped parsley before serving.

SERVES 6

Cream of fennel and leek soup

30 g (1 oz) butter
2 large fennel bulbs, thinly
    sliced
2 leeks, thinly sliced
1 litre (35 fl oz/4 cups) hot
    vegetable or chicken stock
2 rosemary sprigs
1/8 teaspoon ground nutmeg
80 g (2¾ oz/1/3 cup) sour cream

25 g (1 oz/¼ cup) finely grated
    parmesan cheese
1 tablespoon oil
1 leek, extra, cut in half
    lengthways, and cut into
    4 cm (1½ inch) lengths
grated parmesan cheese, extra,
    to garnish
sour cream, extra, to garnish

Heat the butter in a large heavy-based saucepan and add the sliced fennel and leek. Cook, covered, over medium heat for 2–3 minutes, stirring occasionally.

Put the hot stock, rosemary sprigs and nutmeg in a saucepan and bring to the boil. Simmer over low heat for about 15 minutes, then remove the rosemary sprigs and add the fennel and leek mixture to the pan.

Transfer the soup to a blender or food processor and blend in batches until smooth. Return to the pan and stir in the sour cream and parmesan. Reheat over medium heat until hot. Season to taste and keep warm.

Heat the oil in a frying pan and cook the extra leek for 2–3 minutes, or until soft but not browned.

Top with the fried leek and garnish with the extra parmesan and sour cream. Serve immediately.

SERVES 6

Chicken, mushroom and Madeira soup

10 g (¼ oz) dried porcini
    mushrooms
25 g (1 oz) butter
1 leek, white part only, thinly
    sliced
250 g (9 oz) pancetta, chopped
200 g (7 oz) Swiss brown
    mushrooms, roughly chopped
300 g (10½ oz) large field
    mushrooms, chopped
2 tablespoons plain
    (all-purpose) flour

125 ml (4 fl oz/½ cup) Madeira
1.25 litres (44 fl oz/5 cups)
    chicken stock
1 tablespoon olive oil
2 chicken breast fillets (about
    200 g/7 oz each)
80 g (2¾ oz/⅓ cup) light sour
    cream
2 teaspoons chopped marjoram,
    plus whole leaves, to garnish

Soak the porcini in 250 ml (9 fl oz/1 cup) boiling water for 20 minutes.

Melt the butter in a large saucepan over medium heat and add the leek and pancetta. Cook for 5 minutes, or until the leek is softened. Add all the mushrooms and the porcini soaking liquid and cook for 10 minutes. Stir in the flour and cook for 1 minute. Add the Madeira and cook, stirring, for 10 minutes. Stir in the stock, bring to the boil, then reduce the heat and simmer for 45 minutes. Cool slightly.

Heat the oil in a frying pan and cook the chicken for 4–5 minutes each side, or until cooked through. Remove from the pan and thinly slice.

Blend the soup until smooth. Return to the saucepan, add the sour cream and chopped marjoram and stir over medium heat for about 1–2 minutes to warm through. Season. Top with the chicken and garnish with marjoram.

SERVES 4

Creamy clam soup

1.75 kg (4 lb) clams, cleaned
50 g (1¾ oz) butter
1 onion, chopped
1 celery stalk, chopped
1 large carrot, chopped
1 large leek, sliced into rings
250 g (9 oz) swede (rutabaga), diced
800 ml–1 litre (28–35 fl oz) fish stock

1 bay leaf
75 g (2½ oz/⅓ cup) medium- or short-grain rice
200 ml (7 fl oz) pouring (whipping) cream
3 tablespoons finely chopped flat-leaf (Italian) parsley

Fish substitution
pipis

Put the clams and 250 ml (9 fl oz/1 cup) water in a large saucepan. Bring to the boil, then reduce the heat to medium and cover with a tight-fitting lid. Cook for 3–4 minutes, or until the shells open. Strain into a bowl. Add enough stock to make up to 1 litre (35 fl oz/4 cups). Discard any clams that haven't opened. Remove all but eight of the clams from their shells.

Melt the butter in a saucepan. Add the vegetables and cook, covered, over medium heat for 10 minutes, stirring occasionally. Add the stock and bay leaf, bring to the boil, then reduce the heat and simmer for 10 minutes. Add the rice, bring back to the boil, cover and cook over medium heat for 15 minutes, or until the rice and vegetables are tender. Remove from the heat and stir in the clam meat. Remove the bay leaf and allow to cool for 10 minutes.

Purée the soup in a blender until smooth, then return to a saucepan. Stir in the cream and season. Gently reheat the soup. Add the parsley and two clams in the shell to each bowl.

SERVES 4

Sweet potato and pear soup

25 g (1 oz) butter
1 small white onion, finely chopped
750 g (1 lb 10 oz) orange sweet potato,
   peeled and cut into 2 cm (¾ inch) cubes
2 firm pears (500 g/1 lb 2 oz), peeled,
   cored and cut into 2 cm (¾ inch) cubes
750 ml (26 fl oz/3 cups) vegetable or chicken stock
250 ml (9 fl oz/1 cup) pouring (whipping) cream
mint leaves, to garnish

Melt the butter in a saucepan over medium heat. Add the onion and cook for
2–3 minutes, or until softened. Add the sweet potato and pear, and cook, stirring,
for 1–2 minutes. Add the stock, bring to the boil and cook for 20 minutes, or until
the sweet potato and pear are soft.

Cool slightly, then place the mixture in a blender or food processor and blend in
batches until smooth. Return to the pan, stir in the cream and gently reheat
without boiling. Season and garnish with the mint.

SERVES 4

New England
clam chowder

1.5 kg (3 lb 5 oz) clams, cleaned
2 teaspoons oil
3 bacon slices, chopped
1 onion, chopped
1 garlic clove, crushed
750 g (1 lb 10 oz) potatoes, diced

330 ml (11¼ fl oz/1⅓ cups) fish stock
500 ml (17 fl oz/2 cups) milk
125 ml (4 fl oz/½ cup) pouring (whipping) cream
3 tablespoons chopped flat-leaf (Italian) parsley

Put the clams in a large heavy-based saucepan with 250 ml (9 fl oz/1 cup) of water. Cover and simmer for about 4 minutes, or until they open. Discard any that do not open. Strain the liquid through a muslin-lined sieve and reserve. Pull most of the clams out of their shells, leaving a few intact as a garnish.

Heat the oil in a saucepan. Add the bacon, onion and garlic and cook, stirring, over medium heat until the onion is soft and the bacon golden. Add the potato and stir well.

Add enough water to the reserved clam liquid to make 330 ml (11¼ fl oz/ 1⅓ cups) of liquid in total. Pour this and the stock into the saucepan and bring to the boil. Pour in the milk and bring back to the boil. Reduce the heat, cover and simmer for 20 minutes, or until the potato is tender. Uncover and simmer for 10 minutes, or until slightly thickened. Add the cream, clam meat and parsley and season. Heat through gently, but do not allow to boil. Serve with the clams in shells as a garnish.

SERVES 4

Jerusalem artichoke
and roast garlic soup

1 garlic head
40 g (1½ oz) butter
1 tablespoon olive oil
1 onion, chopped
1 leek, white part only, chopped
1 celery stalk, chopped
700 g (1 lb 9 oz) Jerusalem artichokes, peeled and chopped
1 small potato, chopped
1.5 litres (52 fl oz/6 cups) vegetable or chicken stock
olive oil, to serve
finely chopped chives, to garnish

Preheat the oven to 200°C (400°F/Gas 6). Slice the base from the head of garlic, wrap it in foil and roast for 30 minutes, or until soft. When cool enough to handle, remove from the foil and slip the cloves from the skin. Set aside.

Heat the butter and oil in a large heavy-based saucepan over medium heat. Add the onion, leek and celery and a large pinch of salt and cook for 10 minutes, or until soft. Add the Jerusalem artichokes, potato and garlic and cook for a further 10 minutes. Pour in the stock and bring the mixture to the boil. Reduce the heat and simmer for 30 minutes, or until the vegetables are soft.

Purée the mixture in a blender until smooth, and season well. Serve with a drizzle of olive oil and garnish with chives.

SERVES 4

Lobster soup with zucchini and avocado

50 g (1¾ oz) butter
1 garlic clove, crushed
2 French shallots, finely chopped
1 onion, chopped
1 zucchini (courgette), diced
2½ tablespoons dry white wine
400 ml (14 fl oz) fish stock
250 g (9 oz) raw lobster meat, chopped
250 ml (9 fl oz/1 cup) thick (double/heavy) cream

1 avocado, diced
1 tablespoon chopped coriander (cilantro) leaves
1 tablespoon chopped flat-leaf (Italian) parsley
lemon juice, to serve

Fish substitution
crayfish, prawns (shrimp)

Melt the butter in a large saucepan over medium heat. Add the garlic, chopped shallots, onion and zucchini and cook for 8–10 minutes, or until the vegetables are just soft.

Add the wine and bring to the boil, then simmer for 3 minutes. Pour in the stock and bring to the boil again. Reduce the heat to low, add the lobster and simmer for 3–4 minutes, or until the lobster meat is opaque and tinged pink. Gently stir in the cream and season well.

Ladle the soup into four bowls and stir some of the avocado, coriander and parsley into each one. Squeeze a little lemon juice over the soup before serving.

SERVES 4

spicy

Vegetable and lentil soup with spiced yoghurt

2 tablespoons olive oil
1 leek, white part only, chopped
2 garlic cloves, crushed
2 teaspoons curry powder
1 teaspoon ground cumin
1 teaspoon garam masala
1 litre (35 fl oz/4 cups) vegetable stock
1 bay leaf
185 g (6½ oz/1 cup) brown lentils
450 g (1 lb) butternut pumpkin (squash), peeled and cut into 1 cm (½ inch) cubes
2 zucchini (courgettes), cut in half lengthways and sliced
400 g (14 oz) tinned chopped tomatoes
200 g (7 oz) broccoli, cut into small florets
1 small carrot, diced
80 g (2¾ oz/½ cup) peas
1 tablespoon chopped mint

Spiced yoghurt

250 g (9 oz/1 cup) plain yoghurt
1 tablespoon chopped coriander (cilantro) leaves
1 garlic clove, crushed
3 dashes Tabasco sauce

Heat the oil in a saucepan over medium heat. Add the leek and garlic and cook for 4 minutes. Add the curry powder, cumin and garam masala and cook for 1 minute. Add the stock, bay leaf, lentils and pumpkin. Bring to the boil, then reduce the heat and simmer for 10–15 minutes, or until the lentils are tender. Season. Add the zucchini, tomatoes, broccoli, carrot and 500 ml (17 fl oz/2 cups) of water and simmer for 10 minutes, or until the vegetables are tender. Add the peas and simmer for 2–3 minutes.

To make the spiced yoghurt, put the yoghurt, coriander, garlic and Tabasco in a bowl and stir until combined. Serve with the soup and garnish with the mint.

SERVES 6

Spicy pumpkin and coconut soup

1 small red chilli, seeded and chopped
1 stem lemon grass, white part only, sliced
1 teaspoon ground coriander
1 tablespoon chopped fresh ginger
500 ml (17 fl oz/2 cups) vegetable stock
2 tablespoons oil
1 onion, finely chopped
800 g (1 lb 12 oz) pumpkin (squash) flesh, cubed (see Note)
375 ml (13 oz/1½ cups) coconut milk
3 tablespoons chopped coriander (cilantro) leaves
2 teaspoons shaved palm sugar or soft brown sugar
extra coriander (cilantro) leaves, to garnish

Put the chilli, lemon grass, ground coriander, ginger and 2 tablespoons of vegetable stock in a food processor and process until smooth.

Heat the oil in a large saucepan over medium heat. Add the onion and cook for 5 minutes. Add the spice paste and cook, stirring, for 1 minute.

Add the pumpkin and remaining vegetable stock. Bring to the boil, then reduce the heat and simmer, covered, for 15–20 minutes, or until the pumpkin is tender. Cool slightly, then process in a food processor or blender until smooth. Return to the pan, stir in the coconut milk, coriander and palm sugar and simmer until hot. Garnish with the extra coriander leaves.

SERVES 4

NOTE: You will need to buy 1.5 kg (3 lb 5 oz) pumpkin with the skin on to yield 800 g (1 lb 12 oz) flesh.

Tunisian fish soup

3 tablespoons olive oil
1 onion, chopped
1 celery stalk, chopped
4 garlic cloves, crushed
2 tablespoons tomato paste
   (concentrated purée)
1½ teaspoons ground turmeric
1½ teaspoons ground cumin
2 teaspoons harissa
1 litre (35 fl oz/4 cups) fish stock
2 bay leaves
200 g (7 oz/1 cup) orzo or other
   small pasta

500 g (1 lb 2 oz) mixed skinless
   snapper and sea bass fillets,
   cut into bite-sized chunks
2 tablespoons chopped mint,
   plus some extra leaves,
   to garnish
2 tablespoons lemon juice
pitta bread, to serve (optional)

Fish substitution
cod, haddock, ocean perch,
   coral trout

Heat the oil in a large saucepan over medium heat. Add the onion and celery and cook for 8–10 minutes, or until softened. Add the garlic and cook for a further minute. Stir in the tomato paste, turmeric, cumin and harissa and cook, stirring constantly, for an extra 30 seconds.

Pour the fish stock into the saucepan and add the bay leaves. Bring the liquid to the boil, then reduce the heat to low and simmer gently for 15 minutes.

Add the orzo to the liquid and cook for 2–3 minutes, or until *al dente*. Drop the fish into the liquid and poach gently for 3–4 minutes, or until the fish is opaque. Stir in the mint and lemon juice and season to taste. Serve with warm pitta bread, if desired. Garnish with mint leaves.

SERVES 6

Japanese prawn, scallop and noodle soup

4 dried shiitake mushrooms
100 g (3½ oz) dried soba or
    somen noodles
10 g (¼ oz) sachet bonito-
    flavoured soup stock
75 g (2½ oz) carrot, cut into
    thin batons
150 g (5½ oz) firm tofu, cut
    into cubes
8 scallops, cleaned

16 prawns (shrimp), peeled and
    deveined, tails intact
2 spring onions (scallions),
    finely chopped
1 tablespoon mirin
shichimi togarashi, to serve
    (see Note)

Fish substitution
chunks of firm white fish,
    fish balls

Soak the mushrooms in 300 ml (10½ fl oz) of boiling water for 30 minutes. Cook the noodles in a saucepan of boiling water for 2 minutes, then drain and rinse with cold water. Return the noodles to the pan and cover.

In a saucepan, mix the stock with 1 litre (35 fl oz/4 cups) of water. Drain the mushrooms and add the soaking liquid to the pan. Chop the mushroom caps. Add the mushrooms and carrot to the pan and bring to the boil. Reduce the heat to a simmer and cook for 5 minutes. Add the tofu, scallops, prawns, spring onion and mirin. Simmer for 4 minutes, or until the prawns are pink.

Meanwhile pour hot water over the noodles. Drain. Divide the noodles among four large bowls and pour the soup over, dividing the seafood equally. Serve sprinkled with shichimi togarashi.

SERVES 4

NOTE: Shichimi togarashi is a Japanese condiment.

Split pea and vegetable soup

1 tablespoon peanut or vegetable oil
1 onion, chopped
2 garlic cloves, chopped
1½ teaspoons chopped fresh ginger
1½ tablespoons Madras curry paste
100 g (3½ oz) yellow split peas, rinsed and drained
1 large zucchini (courgette), peeled and chopped
1 large carrot, roughly chopped
170 g (6 oz) button mushrooms, roughly chopped
1 celery stalk, roughly chopped
1 litre (35 fl oz/4 cups) vegetable stock
125 ml (4 fl oz/½ cup) pouring (whipping) cream

Heat the oil in a saucepan, add the onion and cook over low heat for 5 minutes, or until soft. Add the garlic, ginger and curry paste and cook over medium heat for 2 minutes. Stir in the split peas until well coated with paste, then add the zucchini, carrot, mushroom and celery and cook for 2 minutes.

Add the stock, bring to the boil, then reduce the heat and simmer, partly covered, for 1 hour. Remove from the heat and allow to cool slightly.

Transfer the soup to a blender or food processor and process in batches until smooth. Return to the pan, stir in the cream and gently heat until warmed through. Serve with naan bread, if desired.

SERVES 4

Moroccan lamb, chickpea and coriander soup

165 g (5¾ oz/¾ cup) dried chickpeas
1 tablespoon olive oil
850 g (1 lb 14 oz) boned lamb leg, cut into 1 cm
    (½ inch) cubes
1 onion, chopped
2 garlic cloves, crushed
½ teaspoon ground cinnamon
½ teaspoon ground turmeric
½ teaspoon ground ginger
4 tablespoons chopped coriander (cilantro) leaves
800 g (1 lb 12 oz) tinned chopped tomatoes
1 litre (35 fl oz/4 cups) chicken stock
160 g (5¾ oz/⅔ cup) dried red lentils, rinsed
coriander (cilantro) leaves, to garnish

Soak the chickpeas in cold water overnight. Drain and rinse well.

Heat the oil in a large saucepan over high heat and brown the lamb in batches for 2–3 minutes. Reduce the heat to medium, return the lamb to the pan with the onion and garlic and cook for 5 minutes. Add the spices, season and cook for 2 minutes. Add the coriander, tomato, stock and 500 ml (17 fl oz/2 cups) of water and bring to the boil over high heat.

Add the lentils and chickpeas and simmer, covered, over low heat for 1½ hours. Uncover and cook for 30 minutes, or until the lamb is tender and the soup is thick. Season. Garnish with coriander.

SERVES 4–6

Saffron and Jerusalem artichoke soup

1 pinch saffron threads
250 g (9 oz) Jerusalem artichokes
2 tablespoons lemon juice
1 tablespoon olive oil
1 large onion, finely chopped
1 litre (35 fl oz/4 cups) vegetable or chicken stock
3 teaspoons ground cumin
500 g (1 lb 2 oz) desiree potatoes, grated
2 teaspoons lemon juice, extra

Put the saffron threads in a bowl with 2 tablespoons of boiling water and set aside.

Peel and thinly slice the artichokes, dropping the slices into a bowl of water mixed with lemon juice to prevent discolouration.

Heat the oil in a large heavy-based saucepan over medium heat. Add the onion and cook for 2–3 minutes, or until the onion is softened. Bring the stock to the boil in a large saucepan. Add the cumin to the onion mixture and cook for a further 30 seconds, or until fragrant. Add the drained artichokes, potato, saffron mixture, stock and extra lemon juice. Bring to the boil, then reduce the heat and simmer for 15–18 minutes, or until the artichokes are very soft.

Transfer to a blender and process in batches until smooth. Return the soup to the pan and season to taste. Reheat over medium heat and serve immediately.

SERVES 4

Cold spicy roast capsicum soup

4 red capsicums (peppers)
2 teaspoons oil
2 garlic cloves, crushed
4 spring onions (scallions), sliced
1 teaspoon finely chopped seeded chillies
425 g (15 oz) tinned crushed tomatoes
125 ml (4 fl oz/½ cup) chilled vegetable stock
1 teaspoon balsamic vinegar
2 tablespoons chopped basil

Cut the capsicums into quarters and remove the seeds and membrane. Put the capsicums skin side up under a hot grill (broiler) and grill until the skins blacken and blisters. Cool in a plastic bag, then peel away the skin and roughly chop the flesh.

Heat the oil in a small saucepan. Add the garlic, spring onion and chilli and cook over low heat for 1–2 minutes, or until softened.

Transfer to a food processor or blender, and add the capsicum, crushed tomatoes and stock. Blend until smooth, then stir in the vinegar and basil. Season to taste. Refrigerate, then serve cold.

SERVES 4

Carrot and ginger soup

750 ml (26 fl oz/3 cups) vegetable stock
1 tablespoon oil
1 onion, chopped
1 tablespoon grated fresh ginger
1 kg (2 lb 4 oz) carrots, chopped
2 tablespoons chopped coriander (cilantro) leaves

Put the stock in a saucepan and bring to the boil.

Heat the oil in a large heavy-based saucepan over medium heat. Add the onion and ginger and cook for 2 minutes, or until the onion has softened.

Add the stock and carrots. Bring to the boil, then reduce the heat and simmer for 10–15 minutes, or until the carrot is cooked and tender.

Pour into a blender or food processor and process in batches until smooth. Return to the pan and add a little more stock or water if needed.

Stir in the coriander and season to taste. Heat gently before serving.

SERVES 4

Pork congee

300 g (10½ oz/1½ cups) long-
    grain rice, thoroughly rinsed
½ star anise
2 spring onions (scallions),
    white part only
4 x 4 cm (1½ x 1½ inch) piece
    ginger, cut into slices
3.5 litres (118 fl oz/14 cups)
    chicken stock
1 tablespoon peanut oil

2 garlic cloves, crushed
1 teaspoon grated ginger, extra
400 g (14 oz) minced (ground)
    pork
ground white pepper
3 tablespoons light soy sauce
sesame oil, to drizzle
6 fried dough sticks (optional,
    see Note)

Put the rice in a large saucepan with the star anise, spring onions, sliced ginger and chicken stock. Bring to the boil, then reduce the heat to low and simmer for 1½ hours, stirring occasionally.

Heat the oil in a frying pan over high heat. Cook the garlic and grated ginger for 30 seconds. Add the pork and cook for 5 minutes, or until browned, breaking up any lumps with a spoon.

Remove the star anise, spring onions and ginger from the soup and discard. Add the pork mixture and simmer for 10 minutes. Season with white pepper and stir in the soy sauce. Serve with a drizzle of sesame oil and fried dough sticks, if desired.

SERVES 4–6

NOTE: Fried dough sticks are available at Chinese bakeries and speciality shops and are best eaten soon after purchasing. If not, reheat in a 200°C (400°F/Gas 6) oven for 5 minutes, then serve.

Soba noodle and vegetable soup

250 g (9 oz) soba noodles
2 dried shiitake mushrooms
2 litres (70 fl oz/8 cups) vegetable stock
120 g (4 oz) snowpeas (mangetout), cut into strips
2 small carrots, cut into thin 5 cm (2 inch) strips
2 garlic cloves, finely chopped
6 spring onions (scallions), cut into 5 cm (2 inch) lengths
   and thinly sliced lengthways
3 cm (1¼ inch) piece ginger, cut into julienne strips
4 tablespoons soy sauce
3 tablespoons mirin or sake
90 g (3¼ oz/1 cup) bean sprouts, trimmed
coriander (cilantro) leaves, to garnish

Cook the noodles according to the packet instructions. Drain.

Soak the mushrooms in 125 ml (4 fl oz/½ cup) of boiling water until soft. Drain, reserving the liquid. Remove the stalk and slice the mushrooms.

Combine the stock, mushrooms, reserved liquid, snowpeas, carrot, garlic, spring onion and ginger in a large saucepan. Bring slowly to the boil, then reduce the heat to low and simmer for 5 minutes, or until the vegetables are tender. Add the soy sauce, mirin and bean sprouts. Cook for a further 3 minutes.

Divide the noodles among four large serving bowls. Ladle the hot liquid and vegetables over the top and garnish with coriander.

SERVES 4

Spicy tomato soup
with chorizo

500 g (1 lb 2 oz) chorizo sausage
2 tablespoons olive oil
3 onions, halved and sliced
3 garlic cloves, thinly sliced
½ teaspoon ground cumin
1 teaspoon paprika
1–2 small red chillies, seeded and finely chopped
1.5 litres (52 fl oz/6 cups) chicken stock
800 g (1 lb 12 oz) tinned chopped tomatoes
4 tablespoons chopped flat-leaf (Italian) parsley

Fill a large deep frying pan with about 3 cm (1¼ inches) of cold water. Add the chorizo sausage, then bring to the boil over high heat. Reduce the heat and simmer, turning occasionally, for 15 minutes, or until the water evaporates, then continue to cook in any fat left in the pan for 3–4 minutes, or until the chorizo is lightly browned. Allow to cool slightly and break into bite-size pieces.

Heat the oil in a large saucepan over medium heat. Cook the onion and garlic for 5–6 minutes, or until soft. Stir in the cumin and paprika, chilli, chicken stock, tomato and half the parsley. Bring to the boil and add the chorizo. Reduce the heat and simmer for 20 minutes. Stir in the remaining parsley and serve immediately.

SERVES 4–6

Duck, mushrooms and rice noodle broth

3 dried shiitake mushrooms
1 Chinese roast duck (1.5 kg/
   3 lb 5 oz)
500 ml (17 fl oz/2 cups) chicken
   stock
2 tablespoons light soy sauce
1 tablespoon Chinese rice wine
2 teaspoons sugar
400 g (14 oz) fresh flat rice
   noodles

2 tablespoons oil
3 spring onions (scallions),
   thinly sliced
1 teaspoon finely chopped
   ginger
400 g (14 oz) bok choy (pak
   choi), trimmed and leaves
   separated
¼ teaspoon sesame oil

Place the shiitake mushrooms in a bowl, cover with 250 ml (9 fl oz/1 cup) of boiling water and soak for 20 minutes. Drain, reserving the liquid and squeezing the excess liquid from the mushrooms. Discard the woody stems and slice the caps.

Remove the skin and flesh from the roast duck. Discard the fat and carcass. Finely slice the duck meat and the skin.

Place the chicken stock, soy sauce, rice wine, sugar and the reserved mushroom liquid in a saucepan over medium heat. Bring to a simmer and cook for 5 minutes.

Meanwhile, place the rice noodles in a heatproof bowl, cover with boiling water and soak. Gently separate the noodles and drain. Divide among soup bowls.

Heat the oil in a wok over high heat. Add the spring onion, ginger and shiitake mushrooms and cook for several seconds. Transfer to the broth with the bok choy and duck meat and simmer for 1 minute, or until the duck has warmed through. Ladle the soup over the noodles and drizzle sesame oil on each serving.

SERVES 4–6

Spicy Portuguese
chicken soup

2.5 litres (85 fl oz/10 cups) chicken stock
1 onion, cut into thin wedges
1 celery stalk, finely chopped
1 teaspoon grated lemon zest
3 tomatoes, peeled, seeded and chopped
1 mint sprig
1 tablespoon olive oil
2 chicken breast fillets
200 g (7 oz/1 cup) long-grain rice
2 tablespoons lemon juice
2 tablespoons shredded mint

Combine the chicken stock, onion, celery, lemon zest, tomatoes, mint and olive oil in a large saucepan. Slowly bring to the boil, then reduce the heat, add the chicken and simmer gently for 20–25 minutes, or until the chicken is cooked through.

Remove the chicken from the saucepan and discard the mint sprig. Allow the chicken to cool, then thinly slice.

Meanwhile, add the rice to the pan and simmer for 25–30 minutes, or until the rice is tender. Return the sliced chicken to the pan, add the lemon juice and stir for 1–2 minutes, or until the chicken is warmed through. Season and stir through the mint.

SERVES 6

Spicy parsnip soup

1.25 litres (44 fl oz/5 cups) vegetable or chicken stock
30 g (1 oz) butter
1 white onion, cut into quarters and finely sliced
1 leek, finely sliced
500 g (1 lb 2 oz) parsnips, peeled and finely sliced
1 tablespoon Madras curry powder
1 teaspoon ground cumin
315 ml (11 oz/1¼ cups) pouring (whipping) cream (see Note)
10 g (¼ oz/⅓ cup) coriander (cilantro) leaves

Bring the stock to the boil in a saucepan and keep at a low simmer.

Melt the butter in a large saucepan over medium heat. Add the onion, leek and parsnip and cook, covered, for 5 minutes. Add the curry powder and cumin and cook for 1 minute. Stir in the stock and cook, covered, over medium heat for about 10 minutes, or until tender.

Transfer the soup to a blender or food processor and blend in batches until smooth. Return to the pan. Stir in the cream and warm through over low heat. Season to taste and scatter with coriander leaves.

SERVES 6

NOTE: This soup is also delicious without the cream, if you prefer not to add it.

Spicy seafood and roasted corn soup

2 corn cobs (700 g/1 lb 9 oz)
1 tablespoon olive oil
1 red onion, finely chopped
1 small red chilli, finely chopped
½ teaspoon ground allspice
4 vine-ripened tomatoes,
    peeled and finely diced
1.5 litres (52 fl oz/6 cups) fish
    stock or light chicken stock
300 g (10½ oz) boneless firm
    white fish fillets, diced
200 g (7 oz) fresh crab meat

200 g (7 oz) peeled raw prawns
    (shrimp), roughly chopped
1 tablespoon lime juice

Quesadillas
4 flour tortillas (19 cm/7½ inch)
85 g (3 oz/⅔ cup) grated
    cheddar cheese
1 large handful coriander
    (cilantro) leaves
2 tablespoons olive oil

Preheat the oven to 200°C (400°F/Gas 6). Peel back the husks on the corn cobs and remove the silks. Fold the husks back over the corn, put in a baking dish and bake for 1 hour, or until the corn is tender.

Heat the oil in a saucepan over medium heat. Add the onion and cook until soft. Add the chilli and allspice and cook for 1 minute, then add the tomato and stock and bring to the boil. Reduce the heat and simmer, covered, for 45 minutes. Slice off the kernels from the corn cobs, add to the soup and simmer for 15 minutes. Add the fish, crab and prawn meat and simmer for 5 minutes. Add the lime juice.

Meanwhile, to make the quesadillas, top one tortilla with half the cheese and half the coriander. Season, then top with another tortilla. Heat 1 tablespoon of the oil in a frying pan and cook the quesadilla for 30 seconds on each side. Repeat. Cut into wedges and serve with the soup.

SERVES 4

Five-spice duck and somen noodle soup

4 duck breasts, skin on
1 teaspoon Chinese five-spice
1 teaspoon peanut oil
200 g (7 oz) dried somen noodles

Star anise broth
1 litre (35 fl oz/4 cups) chicken stock
3 whole star anise
5 spring onions (scallions), chopped
1 large handful coriander (cilantro) leaves, chopped

Preheat the oven to 200°C (400°F/Gas 6). Trim the duck breast of excess fat, then lightly sprinkle both sides with the Chinese five-spice.

Heat the oil in a large frying pan over medium heat. Add the duck, skin side down, and cook for 2–3 minutes, or until brown and crisp. Turn and cook the other side for 3 minutes. Transfer to a baking tray and cook, skin side up, for a further 8–10 minutes, or until cooked to your liking.

Meanwhile, put the chicken stock and star anise in a small saucepan. Bring to the boil, then reduce the heat and simmer for 5 minutes. Add the spring onion and coriander and simmer for 5 minutes.

Cook the noodles in a saucepan of boiling water for 2 minutes, or until soft. Drain and divide among four bowls. Ladle the broth on the noodles and top each bowl with one sliced duck breast.

SERVES 4

Chickpea, potato and spinach soup

1 litre (35 fl oz/4 cups) vegetable stock
1½ tablespoons olive oil
1 onion, finely chopped
1 large potato, cut into 1.5 cm (⅝ inch) cubes
1½ teaspoons paprika
2 garlic cloves, crushed
400 g (14 oz) tinned chickpeas, drained
1 large tomato, cut into small cubes
50 g (1¾ oz) English spinach, coarsely shredded
25 g (1 oz/¼ cup) grated parmesan cheese

Put the stock in a saucepan, then cover and slowly bring to the boil.

Heat the olive oil in a large heavy-based saucepan. Cook the onion for 2 minutes, or until soft. Add the potato to the onion, and stir in the paprika, garlic and chickpeas. Add the onion mixture to the stock and bring to the boil. Stir in the tomato, and season.

Simmer for 10 minutes, or until the potato is tender. Add the spinach and cook until wilted. Top with parmesan and season to taste.

SERVES 4

hearty

Capsicum, spinach and chickpea soup

1 tablespoon olive oil
8 spring onions (scallions), finely sliced
1 red capsicum (pepper)
1 garlic clove, crushed
1 teaspoon cumin seeds
375 ml (13 fl oz/1½ cups) tomato passata (puréed tomatoes)
750 ml (26 fl oz/3 cups) vegetable or beef stock
300 g (10½ oz) tinned chickpeas, rinsed and drained
2 teaspoons red wine vinegar
1–2 teaspoons sugar
100 g (3½ oz) baby English spinach leaves

Heat the oil in a large heavy-based saucepan over medium heat and stir in the spring onion. Reduce the heat and cook, covered, for 2–3 minutes, or until softened.

Rmove the seeds and membrane from the capsicum and finely dice. Add the capsicum, garlic and cumin seeds to the pan and cook for 1 minute.

Add the passata and stock and bring the mixture to the boil. Reduce the heat and simmer for 10 minutes. Add the chickpeas, vinegar and sugar to the soup and simmer for a further 5 minutes. Stir in the baby spinach and season to taste. Cook until the spinach begins to wilt. Serve immediately.

SERVES 4

Chicken and
spinach risoni soup

1 tablespoon olive oil
1 leek, quartered lengthways and thinly sliced
2 garlic cloves, crushed
1 teaspoon ground cumin
1.5 litres (52 fl oz/6 cups) chicken stock
2 boneless, skinless chicken breast fillets
205 g (7¼ oz/1 cup) risoni
150 g (5½ oz) baby English spinach leaves, roughly chopped
1 tablespoon chopped dill
2 teaspoons lemon juice

Heat the oil in a large saucepan over low heat. Add the leek and cook for about
8–10 minutes, or until soft. Add the garlic and cumin and cook for 1 minute. Pour
the stock into the pan, increase the heat to high and bring to the boil. Reduce the
heat to low, add the chicken fillets and simmer, covered, for 8 minutes. Remove
the chicken from the broth, allow to cool slightly, then shred.

Stir the risoni into the broth and simmer for 12 minutes, or until *al dente*.

Return the chicken to the broth along with the spinach and dill. Simmer for
2 minutes, or until the spinach has wilted. Stir in the lemon juice and season
to taste.

SERVES 4

Pasta and bean soup

200 g (7 oz/1 cup) dried borlotti
    beans
3 tablespoons olive oil
90 g (3¼ oz) pancetta or bacon,
    finely diced
1 onion, finely chopped
2 garlic cloves, crushed
1 celery stalk, thinly sliced
1 carrot, diced
1 bay leaf
1 rosemary sprig
1 flat-leaf (Italian) parsley sprig

400 g (14 oz) tinned chopped
    tomatoes, drained
1.625 litres (55 fl oz/6½ cups)
    vegetable stock
2 tablespoons finely chopped
    flat-leaf (Italian) parsley
150 g (5½ oz) ditalini or other
    small dried pasta
extra virgin olive oil, to drizzle
freshly grated parmesan cheese,
    to serve

Put the borlotti beans in a large bowl, cover with cold water and leave to soak overnight. Drain and rinse.

Heat the oil in a large saucepan over medium heat. Add the pancetta, onion, garlic, celery and carrot and cook for 5 minutes, or until golden. Season with black pepper. Add the bay leaf, rosemary, parsley, tomato, stock and beans and bring to the boil. Reduce the heat and simmer for 1½ hours, or until the beans are tender. Add more boiling water if necessary to maintain the liquid level.

Discard the bay leaf, rosemary and parsley sprigs. Scoop out 250 ml (9 fl oz/1 cup) of the bean mixture and purée in a food processor or blender. Return to the pan, season and add the parsley and pasta. Simmer for 6 minutes, or until the pasta is *al dente*. Remove from the heat and set aside for 10 minutes. Serve drizzled with extra virgin olive oil and garnished with parmesan.

SERVES 4

Broth with ravioli

1.5 litres (52 fl oz/6 cups) vegetable or chicken stock
500 g (1 lb 2 oz) spinach and ricotta ravioli
175 g (6 oz) snowpeas (mangetout), sliced on the diagonal
4 tablespoons chopped flat-leaf (Italian) parsley
4 tablespoons chopped basil
grated parmesan cheese, to garnish

Place the stock in a large heavy-based saucepan and bring to the boil. Add the ravioli and cook for 8–10 minutes, or until the pasta is *al dente*.

Season to taste and stir in the snowpeas, parsley and basil. Sprinkle with grated parmesan just before serving.

SERVES 2

Manhattan-style
seafood chowder

60 g (2¼ oz) butter
3 bacon slices, chopped
2 onions, chopped
2 garlic cloves, finely chopped
2 celery stalks, sliced
3 potatoes, diced
3 teaspoons chopped thyme
1.25 litres (44 fl oz/5 cups) fish
   stock
1 kg (2 lb 4 oz) baby clams
1 tablespoon tomato paste
   (concentrated purée)

400 g (14 oz) tinned chopped
   tomatoes
375 g (13 oz) skinless ling fillets,
   cut into bite-sized pieces
12 large prawns (shrimp),
   peeled and deveined,
   tails intact
2 tablespoons chopped flat-leaf
   (Italian) parsley

Fish substitution
cod, flake, hake

Melt the butter in a saucepan over low heat. Add the bacon, onion, garlic and celery and cook, stirring occasionally, for 5 minutes, or until soft. Add the potato, thyme and 1 litre (35 fl oz/4 cups) of the stock to the saucepan and bring to the boil. Reduce the heat and simmer, covered, for 15 minutes. Pour the remaining stock into a saucepan and bring to the boil. Add the clams, cover and cook for 3–5 minutes, or until they open. Discard any that do not open. Drain the clam liquid through a muslin-lined sieve and add to the soup mixture. Pull most of the clams out of their shells, leaving a few intact to garnish.

Stir the tomato paste and chopped tomatoes into the soup and bring back to the boil. Add the fish, clams and prawns and simmer over low heat for 3 minutes, or until the seafood is cooked. Season and stir in the parsley. Serve garnished with the clams in their shells.

SERVES 4

Mushroom and tortellini soup

1 tablespoon olive oil
175 g (6 oz) small flat mushrooms, sliced
6 spring onions (scallions), sliced
1 small garlic clove, crushed
1.25 litres (44 fl oz/5 cups) vegetable or chicken stock
1 tablespoon port
2 teaspoons Worcestershire sauce
200 g (7 oz) fresh large ricotta tortellini
shaved parmesan cheese, to garnish

Heat the oil in a large heavy-based saucepan over high heat. Add the mushrooms and cook for 2 minutes, browning the mushrooms before turning. Add the spring onion and garlic and cook for a further 1 minute.

Meanwhile, bring the stock to the boil in a separate saucepan. Add the stock, port and Worcestershire sauce to the mushroom mixture and bring to the boil. Add the tortellini and simmer for 8 minutes, or until the tortellini is *al dente*.

Season to taste and serve topped with shaved parmesan.

SERVES 4

Seafood soup with rouille

Rouille

1 cooked russet potato, peeled and diced

1 red capsicum (pepper), grilled and peeled

2 garlic cloves, chopped

1 egg yolk

125 ml (4 fl oz/½ cup) olive oil

1 litre (35 fl oz/4 cups) fish stock

½ teaspoon saffron threads

4 thyme sprigs

5 cm (2 inch) piece orange peel

1 small baguette

olive oil, for brushing

300 g (10½ oz) salmon fillet, cut into 4 pieces

300 g (10½ oz) ling fillet, cut into 4 pieces

1 squid tube, cleaned and cut into rings

8 raw king prawns, shelled and deveined

To make the rouille, place the potato, capsicum, garlic and egg yolk in a food processor and process until smooth. With the motor running, gradually add the olive oil until the mixture has the consistency of mayonnaise.

Preheat the oven to 180°C (350°F/Gas 4). Put the stock in a large saucepan and bring to the boil. Add the saffron, thyme and orange peel. Remove from the heat and leave to stand for 10 minutes to allow the flavours to infuse.

Meanwhile, cut the baguette into 1 cm (½ inch) slices. Brush with oil and put on a baking tray. Bake for 10 minutes, or until crisp and golden.

Strain the stock and return to the boil, then add the salmon, ling, squid rings and prawns. Remove the stock from the heat and leave for 2 minutes, or until the seafood is cooked. Serve with the rouille and croutons.

SERVES 4

Zuppa di faggioli

800 g (1 lb 12 oz) tinned
    cannellini beans
1 tablespoon extra virgin olive oil
1 leek, finely chopped
2 garlic cloves, crushed
1 teaspoon thyme leaves
2 celery stalks, diced
1 carrot, diced
1 kg (2 lb 4 oz) silverbeet (Swiss
    chard), trimmed and roughly
    chopped

1 ripe tomato, diced
1 litre (35 fl oz/4 cups)
    vegetable stock
2 small crusty rolls, each cut
    into 4 slices
2 teaspoons balsamic vinegar
35 g (1¼ oz/⅓ cup) finely
    grated parmesan cheese

Put half of the cannellini beans and half of the liquid in a blender or food processor and blend until smooth. Drain the remaining beans and set aside.

Heat the oil in a large heavy-based saucepan over medium heat. Add the leek, garlic and thyme and cook for 2–3 minutes, or until soft and aromatic. Add the celery, carrot, silverbeet and tomato and cook for a further 2–3 minutes, or until the silverbeet has wilted. Heat the stock in a separate saucepan.

Stir the puréed cannellini beans and stock into the vegetable mixture. Bring to the boil, then reduce the heat and simmer for 5–10 minutes, or until the vegetables are tender. Add the drained beans and stir until heated through. Season to taste.

Arrange 2 slices of bread in the base of each soup bowl. Stir the balsamic vinegar into the soup and ladle over the bread. Serve topped with grated parmesan.

SERVES 4

Chunky fish soup with bacon and dumplings

2 tablespoons olive oil
1 onion, chopped
1 small red capsicum (pepper), chopped
1 small zucchini (courgette), diced
150 g (5½ oz) smoked bacon, chopped
1 garlic clove, crushed
2 tablespoons paprika
400 g (14 oz) tinned chopped tomatoes
400 g (14 oz) tinned chickpeas

450 g (1 lb) skinless pike fillet, cut into large pieces
2 tablespoons chopped flat-leaf (Italian) parsley

Dumplings
75 g (2½ oz) self-raising flour
1 egg, lightly beaten
1½ tablespoons milk
2 teaspoons finely chopped marjoram

Fish substitution
bream, char, trout

Heat the oil in a saucepan over low heat. Add the onion and cook for 8 minutes, or until softened. Add the capsicum, zucchini, bacon and garlic and cook over medium heat for 5 minutes, stirring occasionally.

Meanwhile, to make the dumplings, combine the flour, egg, milk and marjoram in a bowl and mix with a wooden spoon.

Add the paprika, tomato, chickpeas and 800 ml (28 fl oz) water to the vegetables. Bring the liquid to the boil, then reduce the heat to low and simmer gently for 10 minutes, or until thickened slightly. Using two tablespoons to help you form the dumplings, add six rounds of the dumpling mixture to the soup. Poach for 2 minutes, then slide the pieces of fish into the liquid. Poach for a further 2–3 minutes, or until the fish is cooked. Season to taste and sprinkle with parsley

SERVES 6

Minestrone alla Milanese

225 g (8 oz) dried borlotti beans
55 g (2 oz) butter
1 onion, finely chopped
1 garlic clove, finely chopped
3 tablespoons flat-leaf (Italian) parsley, finely chopped
2 sage leaves
100 g (3½ oz) pancetta, cubed
2 celery stalks, halved, then sliced
2 carrots, sliced
3 potatoes, peeled but left whole
1 teaspoon tomato paste (concentrated purée)
400 g (14 oz) tinned chopped tomatoes
8 basil leaves
3 litres (101 fl oz/12 cups) chicken or vegetable stock
2 zucchini (courgettes), sliced
225 g (8 oz) shelled peas
125 g (4½ oz) runner beans, cut into 4 cm (1½ inch) lengths
¼ cabbage, shredded
220 g (7¾ oz/1 cup) risotto rice
grated parmesan cheese, to serve

Put the dried beans in a large bowl, cover with cold water and soak overnight. Drain and rinse under cold water.

Melt the butter in a saucepan and add the onion, garlic, parsley, sage and pancetta. Cook over low heat, stirring until the onion is soft.

Add the celery, carrot and potatoes, and cook for 5 minutes. Stir in the tomato paste, tomatoes, basil and borlotti beans. Season with pepper. Add the stock and bring slowly to the boil. Cover and leave to simmer for 2 hours, stirring once or twice.

If the potatoes have not broken up, roughly break them with a fork. Season to taste and add the zucchini, peas, runner beans, cabbage and rice. Simmer until the rice is cooked. Serve with the parmesan cheese.

SERVES 6

Goulash soup
with dumplings

3 tablespoons olive oil

1 kg (2 lb 4 oz) chuck steak, cut into 1 cm (½ inch) cubes

2 large onions, chopped

3 garlic cloves, crushed

1 green capsicum (pepper), chopped

1½ teaspoons caraway seeds, ground

3 tablespoons sweet paprika

¼ teaspoon ground nutmeg

pinch cayenne pepper

½ teaspoon sea salt

400 g (14 oz) tinned chopped tomatoes

2 litres (70 fl oz/8 cups) chicken stock

350 g (12 oz) potatoes, diced

1 green capsicum (pepper), julienned

2 tablespoons sour cream

Dumplings

1 egg

3 tablespoons finely grated parmesan cheese

75 g (2½ oz/⅔ cup) self-raising flour

pinch cayenne pepper

Heat half the oil in a saucepan over medium heat. Cook the beef in batches for 1–2 minutes. Remove and set aside. Heat the remaining oil in the pan over low heat. Add the onion, garlic and chopped capsicum and cook for 5–6 minutes, or until softened. Stir in the spices and salt. Return the beef to the pan. Stir in the tomato and stock and bring to the boil. Reduce the heat to low and simmer, covered, for 1¼ hours. Add the potato and cook for 30 minutes. Stir in the julienned capsicum and sour cream.

To make the dumplings, combine the ingredients and a pinch of salt to form a dough. Turn onto a floured surface and knead for 5 minutes. Roll ½ teaspoonfuls of the dough into balls, drop into the soup and cook for 6 minutes.

SERVES 4–6

Spaghetti and meatball soup

150 g (5½ oz) spaghetti, broken into 8 cm (3 inch) lengths
1.5 litres (52 fl oz/6 cups) beef stock
3 teaspoons tomato paste (concentrated purée)
400 g (14 oz) tinned chopped tomatoes
3 tablespoons basil leaves, torn
shaved parmesan cheese, to garnish

Meatballs
1 tablespoon oil
1 onion, finely chopped
2 garlic cloves, crushed
500 g (1 lb 2 oz) lean minced (ground) beef
3 tablespoons finely chopped flat-leaf (Italian) parsley
3 tablespoons fresh breadcrumbs
2 tablespoons finely grated parmesan cheese
1 egg, lightly beaten

Cook the spaghetti in a large saucepan of boiling water according to packet instructions until *al dente*. Drain. Put the stock and 500 ml (17 fl oz/2 cups) of water in a large saucepan and slowly bring to a simmer.

Meanwhile, to make the meatballs, heat the oil in a frying pan over medium heat. Cook the onion for 2 minutes, or until soft. Add the garlic. Cook for 30 seconds. Allow to cool. Combine the beef parsley, breadcrumbs, parmesan, egg, the onion mixture and season. Roll a heaped teaspoon of mixture into a ball, making 40 balls.

Stir the tomato paste and tomato into the beef stock and simmer for 2–3 minutes. Drop in the meatballs, return to a simmer and cook for 10 minutes, or until cooked through. Stir in the spaghetti and basil to warm through. Season and top with shaved parmesan.

SERVES 4

Winter lamb shank soup

1 tablespoon olive oil
1.25 kg (2 lb 12 oz) lamb shanks
2 onions, chopped
4 garlic cloves, chopped
250 ml (9 fl oz/1 cup) red wine
2 bay leaves
1 tablespoon chopped rosemary
2.5 litres (85 fl oz/10 cups) beef
   stock
425 g (15 oz) tinned crushed
   tomatoes

165 g (5¾ oz/¾ cup) pearl
   barley, rinsed and drained
1 large carrot, diced
1 potato, diced
1 turnip, diced
1 parsnip, diced
2 tablespoons redcurrant jelly
   (optional)

Heat the oil in a large saucepan over high heat. Cook the lamb shanks for 2–3 minutes, or until brown. Remove from the pan.

Add the onion to the pan and cook over low heat for 8 minutes, or until soft. Add the garlic and cook for 30 seconds, then add the wine and simmer for 5 minutes.

Add the shanks, bay leaves, half the rosemary and 1.5 litres (52 fl oz/6 cups) of the stock to the pan. Season. Bring to the boil over high heat. Reduce the heat and simmer, covered, for 2 hours, or until the meat falls off the bone. Remove the shanks and cool slightly.

Remove the meat off the bone and roughly chop. Add to the broth with the tomato, barley, the remaining rosemary and stock and simmer for 30 minutes. Add the vegetables and cook for 1 hour, or until the barley is tender. Remove the bay leaves, then stir in the redcurrant jelly.

SERVES 4

Silverbeet and risoni soup with gruyère croutons

30 g (1 oz) butter
1 large onion, finely chopped
1 garlic clove, crushed
2 litres (70 fl oz/8 cups) vegetable or chicken stock
200 g (7 oz/1 cup) risoni
½ baguette, cut into 6 slices
15 g (½ oz) butter, extra, melted
1 teaspoon Dijon mustard
50 g (1¾ oz) gruyère cheese, coarsely grated
500 g (1 lb 2 oz) silverbeet (Swiss chard), shredded
30 g (1 oz) basil, torn

Heat the butter in a large heavy-based saucepan over medium heat. Add the onion and garlic and cook for 2–3 minutes, or until the onionis softened.

Meanwhile, put the stock in a large saucepan and bring to the boil.

Add the stock to the onion mixture and bring to the boil. Add the risoni, reduce the heat and simmer for 8 minutes, stirring occasionally.

Meanwhile, put the baguette slices in a single layer on a baking tray and cook under a preheated grill (broiler) until golden brown on one side. Turn the slices over and brush with the combined melted butter and mustard. Top with the gruyère and grill until the cheese has melted.

Add the silverbeet and basil to the risoni mixture and simmer for about 1 minute, or until the risoni is *al dente*. Season and serve with the gruyère croutons.

SERVES 6

Tomato and pasta soup

1.25 litres (44 fl oz/5 cups) vegetable or chicken stock
90 g (3¼ oz/1 cup) spiral pasta
2 carrots, sliced
1 zucchini (courgette), sliced
4 ripe tomatoes, roughly chopped
2 tablespoons shredded basil

Place the stock in a heavy-based saucepan and bring to the boil. Reduce the heat, add the pasta, carrot and zucchini and cook for about 5–10 minutes, or until the pasta is *al dente*.

Add the tomato and heat through gently for a few minutes. Season to taste.

Serve the soup sprinkled with the basil over the top.

SERVES 4

Hearty seafood soup

2 tablespoons dried shrimp
3 tablespoons olive oil
1 large onion, finely chopped
3 garlic cloves, crushed
1 small red chilli, deseeded and finely chopped
1 teaspoon finely grated fresh ginger
3 tablespoons crunchy peanut butter
800 g (1 lb 12 oz) tinned chopped tomatoes
50 g (1¾ oz) creamed coconut, chopped
400 ml (14 fl oz) coconut milk
generous pinch of ground cloves
4 tablespoons chopped coriander (cilantro) leaves
700 g (1 lb 9 oz) swordfish, cut into large chunks
100 g (3½ oz) small prawns (shrimp), peeled and deveined
2 tablespoons chopped cashew nuts

Fish substitution
marlin, tuna, monkfish

Soak the dried shrimp in boiling water for 10 minutes, then drain.

Heat the oil in a saucepan over medium heat. Cook the onion for 5 minutes. Add the garlic, chilli and ginger and cook for 2 minutes. Stir in the dried shrimp, peanut butter, tomato, creamed coconut, coconut milk, ground cloves and half of the coriander. Bring the mixture to the boil and simmer gently for 10 minutes. Remove from the heat, allow to cool slightly, then tip the sauce into a food processor or blender and blend until thick and smooth.

Return the sauce to the pan over medium heat. Add the swordfish and cook for 2 minutes, then add the prawns and continue to simmer until all the seafood is cooked — the prawns will be pink and the fish opaque. Serve with the cashews and remaining coriander sprinkled over the top.

SERVES 4

Tomato bread soup

750 g (1 lb 10 oz) vine-ripened tomatoes
1 loaf day-old crusty Italian bread
1 tablespoon olive oil
3 garlic cloves, crushed
1 tablespoon tomato paste (concentrated purée)
1.25 litres (44 fl oz/5 cups) hot vegetable stock
4 tablespoons torn basil leaves
2–3 tablespoons extra virgin olive oil
extra virgin olive oil, extra, to serve

Score a cross in the base of each tomato. Put in a bowl of boiling water for 1 minute, then plunge into cold water and peel the skin away from the cross. Cut the tomatoes in half and scoop out the seeds with a teaspoon. Chop the tomato flesh.

Remove most of the crust from the bread and discard. Cut the bread into 3 cm (1¼ inch) pieces.

Heat the oil in a large saucepan over medium heat. Add the garlic, tomato and tomato paste, then reduce the heat and simmer, stirring occasionally, for about 10–15 minutes, or until reduced and thickened. Add the stock and bring to the boil, stirring for 2–3 minutes. Reduce the heat to medium, add the bread pieces and cook, stirring, for 5 minutes, or until the bread softens and absorbs most of the liquid. Add more stock or water if necessary.

Stir in the torn basil leaves and extra virgin olive oil, and leave for 5 minutes to allow the flavours to develop. Drizzle with a little extra virgin olive oil to serve.

SERVES 4

Beef ball and white bean soup

600 g (1 lb 5 oz) minced (ground) beef
2 garlic cloves, crushed
1 tablespoon flat-leaf (Italian) parsley, finely chopped
large pinch ground cinnamon
large pinch freshly grated nutmeg
2 eggs, lightly beaten

1.5 litres (52 fl oz/6 cups) beef stock
2 carrots, thinly sliced
800 g (1 lb 12 oz) tinned white beans, drained
½ savoy cabbage, finely shredded
grated parmesan cheese, to serve

Put the beef in a bowl with the garlic, parsley, cinnamon, nutmeg and half of the egg. Mix to combine and season well. If the mixture is dry, add the rest of the egg — it needs to be sticky enough so that forming small balls is easy.

Roll the beef mixture into small balls — they should be small enough to scoop up on a spoon and eat in one mouthful.

Put the beef stock and the carrot in a saucepan and bring to the boil. Add the meatballs, one at a time, and reduce the heat. Simmer for 3 minutes. Add the beans and cabbage and cook for a further 4–5 minutes. Season to taste. Serve with grated parmesan.

SERVES 4

index

First published in 2008 by Murdoch Books Pty Limited

Murdoch Books Australia
Pier 8/9, 23 Hickson Road
Millers Point NSW 2000
Phone: +61 (0) 2 8220 2000
Fax: +61 (0) 2 8220 2558
www.murdochbooks.com.au

Murdoch Books UK Limited
Erico House, 6th Floor
93–99 Upper Richmond Road,
Putney, London SW15 2TG
Phone: +44 (0) 20 8785 5995
Fax: +44 (0) 20 8785 5985
www.murdochbooks.co.uk

Chief Executive: Juliet Rogers
Publishing Director: Kay Scarlett

Design Manager: Vivien Valk
Project manager and editor: Gordana Trifunovic
Design concept: Alex Frampton
Designer: Susanne Geppert
Production: Nikla Martin
Introduction text: Leanne Kitchen
Recipes developed by the Murdoch Books Test Kitchen

Printed by Sing Cheong Printing Co. Ltd in 2008. PRINTED IN HONG KONG.

ISBN 9781741961027 (pbk.).
A catalogue record for this book is available from the British Library.

IMPORTANT: Those who might be at risk from the effects of salmonella poisoning (the elderly, pregnant women, young children and those suffering from immune deficiency diseases) should consult their doctor with any concerns about eating raw eggs.

CONVERSION GUIDE: You may find cooking times vary depending on the oven you are using. For fan-forced ovens, as a general rule, set the oven temperature to 20°C (35°F) lower than indicated in the recipe.